Incomprehensible Demoralization

Incomprehensible Demoralization

An Addict Pharmacist's
Journey to Recovery

Jared Combs

To order additional copies of this book, contact:
Xlibris Corporation
1-888-795-4274
www.Xlibris.com
Orders@Xlibris.com
50051

CONTENTS

Special thanks to the following people (in no particular order) for their support that made publishing this book possible:

Eric Deskins
Janie and Randy Hackney
Dorathea Andrews
Michael Ingram
Eric Brewer
George Fitz
John McGregor
Todd Tipton
Christy Taylor
Gerry Gevedon
Allison Balko
Becky Reagan
John Armitstead
Steve Sitzler
Jill Jones
Karen Maples
Allen Rhodes
Larry Hawkins
Brian Garland
Kenny and Margie Bowling
John Jeff Combs
Steve Miniard
John (Bo) Wallace
Woodson Reynolds
Robin Reed

Special thanks to the following people for loving me through the rough times: My wife Darcey, Mom and Dad, my brother Eric, my sister Michelle and her husband Kerry, CC Cinnamond, and Mark Miller.

Worth a second mention: Loving thanks to my beautiful, loving, God-centered, and tough-as-nails wife Darcey for going to hell and back with me.

FOREWORD

My name is Brian, and I am a grateful recovering alcoholic and drug addict. Wow . . . there it is . . . I said it for any who read this to know. It was, once upon a time, a deep dark secret. It was a secret even I didn't know or comprehend. How can that be? you may say. Well, I say, let me share with you this definition of *alcoholism* (addiction) by Fr. Vernon Johnson:

> Alcoholism/addiction is a disease, the very nature of which renders the victim incapable of recognizing the severity of the symptoms, the progression of the disease or of accepting any ordinary offers of help.

Jared, the author of this story—this autobiography, this horror story, this tale of his journey into recovery—is an alcoholic/addict. He is a husband and a father. He is a man with a primary chronic disease that is progressive. It is also a fatal disease if left untreated. Jared is a friend, a mentor, a sponsor, and—oh, by the way—a pharmacist. He is someone who held the keys to the "candy store," if you will.

He gives his story the title *Incomprehensible Demoralization*. Big words these. He tells us in his story where he got them, yes, but what do they mean? Well, let me share with you what I found. *Incomprehensible*: difficult to understand or comprehend, impossible to know or fathom, not clear to the mind. I would say that it means to me that I/we cannot "think" our way out of this. *Demoralization*: a state of disorder and confusion. Wow, disorder and confusion for sure!

It is said in the rooms of recovery that those with this disease—this "dis-ease"—suffer from a type of insanity. It is described as doing the same things over and over and expecting different results. Remember in the definition from Father Johnson how we are incapable of recognizing the severity of the symptoms—and goodness, does he tell us what it was like, the progression of the disease—you'll surely recognize the insanity as he continued to use even when the consequences became more and more consequential, and how he rebuffed offers of help from those who were affected by his disease. So how do we—those of us who are afflicted—get better?

Jared leads by the hand and walks us along the path he took through his incomprehensible demoralization on his journey that led to his discovery that he had to surrender his life in order to win, in order to stay alive. The day Jared surrendered—the day he gave up thinking he could stop by himself, the day he asked God to help him—is the day he reached out and accepted the gift of sobriety, that grace, that unmerited gift, that was offered to him. Jared came to believe through that surrender that a power greater than himself could restore him to sanity. This is the "what happened" part of what an alcoholic is tasked to do when sharing their story—tell what it was like, what happened, and what it is like now.

Jared shares with us just what is meant by a daily reprieve from this disease, contingent on the maintenance of his spiritual condition, i.e., the relationship that he has with the god of his understanding.

Jared writes in his intro that "hope is powerful." Hope is something on which many of us early in our recovery had given up. We'd given up on having hope until we entered the fellowship of recovering people found in the rooms of AA (Alcoholics Anonymous) or NA (Narcotics Anonymous) or one of the other twelve-step recovery programs. One of the blessings that comes with the gift of sobriety found in a twelve-step recovery is the sharing by others in the fellowship of their experience, strength, and *hope*. Yes, there is hope for those who are afflicted with this disease. Do what is suggested in what is affectionately known as the Big Book, i.e., the book *Alcoholics Anonymous* we are told and life can be okay, as I like to say, one day at a time.

We learn, as did Jared, how to clean up the wreckage of our past. We learn, as did Jared, how to make amends to those who were and are affected by our disease. We learn how to maintain our recovery one day at a time as there is no cure for this disease.

I stay clean and sober one day at a time as does Jared by not using. We've both managed to string together a number of twenty-four-hour periods of abstinence from whatever chemical substances we used to alter our thinking. Abstinence helps us avoid triggering the physical allergy, and regular attendance at twelve-step meetings helps us with the mental obsession we had with the substances. If I continue, and if Jared continues to do what we've been taught works the best for the most with this disease, we—each of us—can be okay today also.

May you find in this book some experience, strength, and hope that may help you some day in some way. The years I've worked with other addicts and alcoholics both in my professional life and in my personal life have led me to love the person and loathe the disease. So in closing, let me say that I cannot ask the god of my understanding for anything more than being okay today. I do, in my daily meditations, ask God to help me each day to stay sober and to be of maximum service to God and to my fellows. In this, I truly believe. Peace be with you.

Brian Fingerson, RPh
KY Professionals Recovery Network
3 May 2008

INTRO TO INSANITY

We alcoholics are men and women who have lost the ability to control our drinking. We know that no real alcoholic ever recovers control. All of us felt at times that we were regaining control, but such intervals—usually brief—were inevitably followed by still less control, which led in time to pitiful and incomprehensible demoralization.

—*Alcoholics Anonymous*, chapter 3,
"More About Alcoholism"

The day everything changed, I found myself alone in a jail cell. I had just gotten arrested for the second time in a week: my fourth alcohol-and-drug arrest altogether. This was my second job as a pharmacist and the second time I had been escorted from a place of employment in handcuffs. It became apparent to me at this juncture that *something just wasn't right.*

I paced around and around the cell, crying and praying, praying and crying. I had developed this practice during a previous stay in a similar institution. I found that if I exercised vigorously in this manner, it might increase my chances of sleep at some later point in the evening in this cold, hard, thought-provoking place called jail. Sleep is a good thing when your world has just come crashing down on you, and you find yourself incarcerated, alone, and terrified. It seems the only real peace that you can have at that point. It's the only time that your mind isn't racing at two hundred miles per hour about all the hell and chaos around you. *Will the judge let me out? Will I end up serving time this time? Will my wife divorce me? Will I ever practice pharmacy again?* Something was different this time, truly different. Something came into that cell and granted me peace and some answers—or at least some possible answers. I believe today that it was God.

Most people, when they discover that something is disrupting their lives and causing serious, life-changing problems, will perceive a pattern fairly quickly and put that particular hindrance out of their lives without much hesitation. If eating strawberries continues to cause an allergic reaction each time they eat them, then they discontinue or limit their consumption of strawberries. If peanuts produce anaphylactic, life-threatening reactions, they avoid peanuts, or they could die. It should be a fairly innate mechanism of self-preservation. However, alcoholics subscribe to a perpetual lie to themselves that *this time, it will be different. This time* the strawberries *won't* cause me a rash! Never mind that the last several times we got drunk we predictably did crazy things, pissed people off, got arrested, hurt ourselves, hurt others, wrecked cars, woke up in strange places, lost things, got in fights, etc. Never mind that a good, honest observation of our behavior *clearly* would suggest that drinking and drugging equal problems.

I didn't catch on to this pattern. I continued to think I could successfully drink and use. I just thought I wasn't doing something right. I just needed to switch drinks; if only I could get the right combination of alcohol and narcotics, perhaps that perfect euphoric feeling would return.

I chased that euphoria to the gates of hell, dragging my wife and family behind me. With no real personal knowledge that anything was wrong, my using and drinking continued to jeopardize my life, marriage, and my career while I chased that feeling of ease and comfort I so craved.

But everything can change in one moment of grace. Some of us, for whatever reason, received a gift. It was a gift of willingness more than anything really. This gift from God gave us the ability to put down the chemicals that tried to destroy us and allowed us to find a better way of life. This is the story of my journey. I discovered confidence, boldness, and happiness through the use of alcohol and drugs as a teenager. I continued to chase that elusive pleasure until it took nearly everything from me, including my family, livelihood, freedom, and also my life. When the pain hurt badly enough, I got down on my knees and asked God for help. Help came, although not quite how I had expected it.

As I paced around the cell that day, it hit me, and these words came out of my mouth, "I am an alcoholic and a drug addict, and I don't *have* to keep living this way." I smiled. Yes, I smiled. Ah, a peace settled my racing heart and mind. It was as though all the negative consequences that awaited me were set aside, out of my mind's sight for a while. For those of us in recovery, that's step 1, the biggest and most important step of our recovering lives. A blanket of relief came over me. Like when you have one of those really bad headaches, and you've taken a handful of ibuprofen, and then later, you feel it *just* starting to ease. It's still there, but there's hope that it is going away. That's what I felt at that moment, *hope*. Thank God!—and so I did.

I prayed for God to show me whatever I needed to do to get better. I prayed for God's will to be done in my life. Then I made just a *few* suggestions to God about what that maybe should be. I suggested that surely, it wasn't His will for me to remain in jail. I bet God gets a big laugh out of me sometimes. As if God is in heaven, saying, "Hmmm, I'm just not sure what I should do in this situation . . . Maybe I'll see what Jared thinks." Yeah, right. Jail is where Jared's best thinking got him!

I had earned some frequent flyer miles with the criminal justice system. I knew there was a chance that my family would be finished with me, that my license to practice pharmacy was probably on its way to the shredder, and that my wife was probably ready to divorce me. There was also great potential for jail time in my future with the pattern that I had created. Still, that God-sent glimmer of hope gave me relief and comfort. I knew deep down in my heart that all my madness could stop today. *Hope is powerful.*

"Do you think you have a problem?" asked the judge the next morning over a video arraignment. *Well, let's see, Judge, . . . let me think. I was arrested three years ago for the same crap. I snort sleeping pills during the daytime. I am a pharmacist that eats Lortab like cops eat doughnuts.*

I frequently black out for days at a time. My wife thinks I have a problem, as well as the rest of my family, including my dog. So far, I'm quackin' and walkin' like a duck, Your Honor!

I could hear my mom asking the judge if she could please approach and talk to him. She spoke some words to the judge that I couldn't quite hear, but getting me out of jail and on my way to treatment was the essence of the conversation.

"Yes, sir" was my answer. I meant it. I felt it. I was ready. I was finally ready. My mom heard the promise and sincerity in my voice. She has told me that she felt hopeful that day to hear those defeated words come out of my mouth.

The judge agreed that treatment would be a good idea and demanded that I go directly to treatment upon my release from jail. He said he wasn't letting me out until everything was arranged and the treatment center was ready for me. Mike Spare, a drug-and-alcohol counselor in my hometown of Hazard, Kentucky had become our family counselor and friend. He declared that he would take full responsibility for me, and that I was officially under his care until being admitted to inpatient treatment. He was sticking his neck out for me so that I could get released immediately. Mike was Darcey's counselor for her depression and eating disorders, my counselor for my alcoholism/addiction (which I had previously denied having), and our family counselor for our marriage. We had a few issues.

I was on my way to a drug-and-alcohol treatment facility outside Nashville within a couple days. I began packing some clothes at home. While gathering things from the closet, I collapsed into a pile of dirty clothes, crying. The immense fear and reality of my situation suddenly hit me, and I came unraveled. I was terrified and defeated. I was afraid of treatment, afraid of sobriety, and afraid of the future. I had no income. I had no pharmacy license. My wife, joining me in the heap of laundry, held me and assured me that it was going to be okay. It was just words, of course. She was just as scared as I was. Her story would be a whole other book. Why she stuck around is beyond me. God must have shared a little hope with her too. Hope is powerful.

Most people think of defeat as a bad thing. For alcoholics and addicts, who can be quite stubborn, it's a good thing. It's an opportunity for a new beginning. It's good when we realize and accept that we have been defeated by drugs and alcohol, because it's usually the only way we will seek out a solution. How many guys show up at an AA meeting in a convertible Jaguar or Mercedes, with a fat bank account, no debt or criminal record, and perfectly groomed, saying, "Everything's great in my life . . . I just thought I'd check out this awesome AA fellowship and have a cup of coffee with you guys"? It just doesn't happen that way. Alcoholics have a high tolerance for pain, so we normally come crawling into AA with our asses hanging off. I had asphalt burns on my face, a black eye, a criminal record, and a very confused and angry wife. My financial situation was *broke*. Broke, that is, except for the ten thousand dollars of "run money" that Darcey had secretly stored away in the event she decided to make a run for it and leave me. I believe this had been a recommendation from her counselor, and a damn good one too.

When I refer to simply alcoholism or drinking, you may assume that I mean alcoholism, addiction, drinking, and/or using. It's all the same to me. Alcohol is a drug. Drugs are just a solid form of alcohol to me. Using is drinking, and drinking is using. Whether snorting pills, drinking alcohol, or shoving poisonous spiders up one's butt, the terms will be used interchangeably throughout this book.

In my recovery today, I am given a daily reprieve from this insanity, contingent on the maintenance of my spiritual condition. Today I have a life that has purpose, love, and direction.

Read on and be entertained as I tell you what it was like before, what happened, and what it's like now as I trudge through this terminal, sexually transmitted disease called life.

KEYS TO THE CANDY STORE AND THE SPIRITUAL EXPERIENCE

In 1996, I became a licensed pharmacist. In that one year, I graduated from school, got my pharmacist's license, married Darcey, bought a house, got a real job, and had the keys to the candy store handed to me. I had experimented with pharmaceuticals in high school and college, but not to any great extent. It all seemed to happen in a very short time.

On Saturday, June 8, 1996, Darcey and I said our vows at the Presbyterian Church in Hazard. It was beautiful. The bridesmaids were stunning, and the groomsmen were handsomely decked out in their tuxedos. Flowers and candles adorned the church, and there was standing room only of friends and family. Darcey was a vision of an angel in her long white dress. I know these things because I saw pictures and video. I have no firsthand memory of the event, I am sad and ashamed to say. I had too much Xanax in my system to be able to come away with many memories.

The next day we left for our honeymoon, a cruise through the western Caribbean, with stops in Grand Cayman, Cozumel, Jamaica, and Haiti. I boarded Royal Caribbean's *Majesty of the Seas* with my new bride and an assortment of pills. I had Xanax, Valium, and a few others for the specific purpose of relaxing while on vacation. I recall getting on the massive boat and checking in our stateroom. After that, the memories get very spotty. Every day while Darcey would go to the ship's gym, I would sit by the pool and get drunk. Every night before dinner, I would lock myself in the bathroom and snort Xanax and various other pills while pretending to shave or shower. One of our stops was Cozumel, Mexico. We went snorkeling near a beach close to the port. After an uneventful and disappointing excursion due to poor visibility and lack of any interesting sights, we came out of the water. There was a vender right on the beach with some lovely cold Corona. I grabbed two beers and headed back to the spot where our towels reserved us a patch of sand. Darcey was giving me the look. It was that passive-aggressive look that quietly radiated disappointment, resentment, anger, and bitterness. Apparently there was a certain time of day before which it was completely unacceptable to drink alcoholic beverages once one is married. I was unaware of this rule. Darcey stormed off back to the boat. I decided to stay and finish my beer first—and perhaps several more. On my way back to the ship, I stopped and bought her a designer purse from the duty-free shops in hopes that it might smooth things out for us. It helped a bit, but was not curative. I eventually had to promise to abstain from any alcoholic beverages before noon.

That honeymoon would set the stage for my behavior during the next several years. At the time, I would have rationalized my behavior by defining the trip as one of those special occasions where there are no rules governing drinking and partying. Occasions such as vacations, certain holidays, and weekend getaways were fair game to relax and unwind, using whatever I could get my hands on without any feelings of guilt or moral obligation. My wife didn't subscribe to this same belief.

Darcey and I continued to have more and more arguments and outright fights over my drinking as the days went by. The increased frequency and quantity of my drinking and the resolute dedication to drinking made her quite nervous. She could sense a problem budding. At this point, I threw occasional pharmaceuticals into the mix, but she didn't know about these.

I thought that she was just a nagging wife. I began to limit and hide my drinking as much as I could in order to keep peace. To me, this was simply a part of marriage. Didn't all couples argue regularly over alcohol consumption? Wasn't it the wife's job to nag about these things and mandate limitations? This may sound like I am trying to be humorous, but that is truly what I thought.

Most importantly, at this point in my life, I discovered what peace and tranquility could be had from the ingestion of a Lortab while at work. I would discover other things too eventually, but Lortab took my narcotic virginity. Nothing speeds up an alcoholic's tumble to his bottom like the addition of drugs to the self-destructive arsenal. As I have mentioned, I had taken drugs before. Somehow though, taking a drug at work without the usual plans for partying opened a new can of worms. It wasn't an attempt to have fun. It was an attempt to cope with a stressful situation. I had arrived at a new level of using. Also, this came with a new level of risk as my job and license were on the line.

I was working at the ARH Hospital clinic in the evenings as the only pharmacist with one technician. It was, at times, stressful to me. Patients were demanding and thankless. My afterwork drinking took on a new fervor to compensate. Why is it people have such high expectations of us pharmacists? They think that a pharmacist should be able to take your prescription from you and almost immediately hand back your medicine to you. A bottle of medicine that is perfectly flawless and accurate. We're supposed to check all your interactions and allergies and deal with your obstinate insurance and then thoroughly counsel you on the medication within a five-minute time span? Why do you people think that fifteen or twenty minutes is too long to complete this process? "How long is it gonna be?" you ask. You'd think we said four days by your reactions. You don't mind waiting thirty minutes on a pizza!

Here's my public service announcement for pharmacy customers nationwide on behalf of retail pharmacists:

- First of all, folks, you ain't the only person in the whole world needing some medicine. Believe it or not, there are other people ahead of you, and they are important too. Have a seat and shut up.
- If you have a taxi waiting out front for you, you are still at the same place in line. It probably wasn't a good idea to *pay* a taxi to wait for you. Have a seat.
- If you have never been here before, don't get huffy with me when I have to ask for your information. All pharmacy computers are not somehow linked up in cyberspace. Get over it.
- If you have an insurance card, I will need to see it at the *beginning* of our conversation, not the end. It's not a credit card

to be swiped at the register. We need the information *before* we fill your prescription. If you hand it to me at the end, I'll have to start all over again.

- If your copay is ten dollars and you thought it should be five, take it up with the insurance. I have no control over your portion of the bill. I repeat, I have no control over your copay. Call your insurance.
- We don't just look at the prescription and then pour from a big bottle to a small bottle and hand it to you. There is a lot of checking and double-checking that goes on in between, and it's a good thing. We like to make sure we put the *right* pills in the *right* bottle. Go find a magazine or a Twinkie.
- If you are one of those people that takes twenty-seven different medications, do not come in at five minutes before closing and expect to leave with your order filled. See you tomorrow. Have a nice day.
- The front counter can hold itself up; please don't lean on it while waiting on your meds. Go find something to do, or go smoke some of your cigarettes while I fill your breathing medications that my tax dollars pay for.

It was a beautiful relationship with pharmaceuticals right from the start. I remember well the day I thought it might be a good idea to take a Lortab while at work. I palmed a tablet as I counted some out to fill a prescription, and popped it in my mouth in our breakroom. An hour later, it had given me patience, knowledge, and love. I was smiling, and angels were singing. My heart felt warm, and my mouth demanded I smile. I no longer hated the patients that were demanding, rude, or stinky. So what if you had a medical card that magically made all your medicines free, yet you have a nicer car and cell phone than me. I'm over it. Those grudges evaporated when my opiate receptors were innervated. I cared about you and your health and well-being now. I felt energetic. I could concentrate better. I was smarter and better looking. It was truly a spiritual experience. I had found the answer, the fountain of youth. This was how people made it through the daily grind of retail pharmacy and its unforgiving customers and long hours. I also felt a trace of superiority and supremacy. I felt better than the people around me, and I relished it. Yet another twisted dimension to this behavior was the adrenaline rush attached to the deceitful nature of the action of using. I could step inside the bathroom, only two sheets of plywood away from my unknowing coworkers, and snort a fat line of today's special. After making some gestures in the mirror to entertain myself (which oddly I still do even clean and sober), I would do a quick nose check to make sure no powder residue was visible, and then step outside to join the pharmaceutically inferior ones. I was energized. I was fueled for a night of pill counting and medical cards! Life was good.

I began to look forward each day to taking narcotics. As soon as I got to work, I would snatch a dose when the opportunity presented itself. It wasn't long until my tolerance increased. I had to take more to get the same happy, joyful effect. Imagine that. I had it under control, I thought. I was merely taking advantage of a fringe benefit of being a pharmacist. Didn't every pharmacist just take from the shelves what they deemed necessary? I honestly assumed that most of them did.

Eventually I began to obsess about it most of my waking hours. As soon as I got out of bed in the morning, I was looking forward to the next opportunity to get high. Naturally, I began taking a supply home with me each day. This initiated the arduous task of using while hiding my use and my drugs from family and coworkers.

Occasionally, I would overshoot that therapeutic window with too much narcotic. My eyelids would droop, my mood would plummet, and I would get very drowsy. To counteract this, I took some type of speed. Ritalin, phentermine, or ephedrine would have me back in action in no time. Of course, this would require some Xanax later in the evening to begin the winding down process.

I decided at some point that I would take them on certain days when I truly *needed* them. I would save them for the busier days like the first of the month when the welfare and social security checks come out, and our volume was up. That didn't last long. That lasted about half a day, and was my first failed attempt to control my using.

In the evenings, I would snort Valium or Xanax to ease me into a restful state before going home and eventually to bed at night. Then I would need something the next morning to get me going again.

The Xanax would sometimes still be affecting me the next day, and I couldn't wake up. Ritalin would take care of that. A line of the pretty blue powder and I was back to life with new vigor and inspiration. I had become dependent on these chemicals for daily activities, and a new chapter had been opened in my life.

On one occasion, I had snorted a few too many Ritalin. I knew this because I could feel my skin crawling, my hair was standing on end, and my heart rate was 150 at rest. It felt like it might just jump right out of my chest or explode within. I could feel it pounding extra hard in my chest and partially up in my neck. I felt panicked, and I got scared that I was going to die. Applying my pharmacology training, I took action. To even things out, I snorted a few too many Xanax with a side order of Tenormin, a heart and blood-pressure medication to slow my heart rate. My heart rate finally came back down, but I slept for about sixteen hours. It's a scary feeling when you feel your heart trying to jump through your rib cage.

Why snort these pills? you ask. I was taking advantage of a physiologic bypassing of the liver. When drugs are taken orally, they go briefly into the bloodstream and then straight to the liver. The liver processes them for elimination from the body. The liver makes a drug more water-soluble and readily eliminated through the kidneys. In layman's terms, it *chews up* a good percentage of the drug before it has the opportunity to get to the site of action. This is called the first-pass effect. By snorting benzos (benzodiazepines—Xanax, Valium, etc.), narcotics, and other drugs, a person bypasses this first-pass effect, achieving a higher level of the drug in the systemic circulation and, therefore, available to act upon the brain. For example, one of my eventual favorite drugs to snort, Sonata, has an oral bioavailability of only 30 percent. So only 3 mg of a 10 mg capsule makes it past the liver. My liver chews up 70 percent of it before it gets to my drug-addicted brain. I hate waste. By snorting, I get 100 percent or at least closer to 100 percent.

Another advantage was that it produced the effect quicker than taking the drug orally. I wanted to feel the rush of the drug seconds after snorting it. It wasn't immediate, but often, I could feel it working before leaving the bathroom in which I was hiding to snort it. Most drugs, taken orally, will take thirty to forty-five minutes before an effect is noticed. Heck, that's longer than it takes to get a prescription filled!

It became a sort of tradition that sometime during the last hour that I worked, my tech and I would split a Xanax line. I would take one back to the bathroom with me and crush it up on the sink. I would snort half of it and then come out and tell her I left the other half for her. On my way home, I would get some beer to top it off and snort some more Xanax. I didn't get the beer every night, but as many nights as I could without pushing Darcey over the edge.

It wasn't long before I was hiding booze and drugs around the house. When I got home at night, Darcey would be preparing for bed. She was an elementary teacher and had to get up early. I would try to not be inebriated when I got home so that Darcey wouldn't give me too much hell. After she went to bed, I would pull out whatever stash I had and get wasted. I kept some vodka inside a peroxide bottle in the downstairs bathroom and, sometimes, a pint or half-pint bottle in the back reservoir of the commode. Drugs would eventually be stashed about everywhere. Frequently, being the nosey, joy-killing wife that she was, she would ease back downstairs and try to catch me enjoying my beverage. I was sure that she did this because she hated me and didn't want me to enjoy my life.

Another stealthy method of detection Darcey employed was the *hug-sniff*. The hug-sniff was probably not invented by Darcey, but she certainly perfected it soon after we got married. As I came in the door from work each evening, she would pretend to be delighted to see me and embrace me pseudolovingly. In one silent maneuver, while pulling away, she inhaled ever so slightly through the nostrils in an attempt to perceive the odor of alcoholic beverages. I soon learned a countermeasure that was only slightly effective. Taking a deep breath before the hug-sniff was initiated, I could sometimes deter detection. She soon learned to counter my countermeasure by initiating conversation while the *hug-sniff* was under way, thereby making it impossible for me to hold my breath without being obvious. Her skills far surpassed mine since she had the distinct advantage of sobriety on her side. Mouthwash or gum was always a dead giveaway, so I cleverly avoided employing these maneuvers.

One night after work in 1997, I decided to take some Soma, a muscle relaxant, right before I left the pharmacy. I had never tried Soma before, and I wanted to try them all! After all, I owed it to the patients to know the effects of all these drugs, didn't I? What kind of pharmacist would I be if I couldn't warn them of the potential dangers to their well-being? Anyway, I took two or three of them. I can't remember which. My ride home from the pharmacy was about fifteen or twenty minutes. Somewhere around the halfway mark, I started feeling the Soma kick in. Turning left at Hardees I felt it taking over my muscles. My arms and head were getting heavy, and a drowsy, relaxing feeling ensued. A quarter mile down the road approaching Pizza Hut, it had all but paralyzed me. At the Pizza Hut intersection, there was a sharp curve of about 140 degrees to the right. I had to slow down to about five miles per hour and ratchet the steering wheel to negotiate the curve. I couldn't move my arms enough to steer, and I couldn't turn my head. I managed to get myself into Pizza Hut's parking lot and shut the car off because by this point, I could barely move. No more Soma while driving, I decided.

Another evening, as part of the ongoing effort to try everything at my disposal, I made the decision to shoot up with some Versed. Versed is in the same family as Valium and is used for anesthesia and preoperative sedation. I had never shot up before and didn't plan on making it a habit or anything like that, but I wanted to try it. I stopped in my driveway and wrapped my belt around my upper arm like I had seen people do in movies and on cable TV. Sure enough, a vein popped up as big as a green bean. I inserted the needle and slowly pushed the drug. Instantly, I was eased into a land of tranquility. I removed the needle, hid it in some garbage, and floated into the house. I had no idea how dangerous this was. Most hospitals will only use this drug in the ICUs or operating rooms because of the danger of respiratory depression. I could have stopped breathing after I went to sleep and never woke up. I didn't die. Apparently, I was a sexual genius that night though. The next day, Darcey made some comments about how much she had enjoyed our frolic in the bed, and she wore a wide smile most of the day. To this day, I don't know what it was that I did so well that night.

As one can imagine, my tolerance gradually increased, and eventually, I had to use something first thing in the mornings to get going. It was kinda like having a stout cup of coffee, except it was powder; and I was snorting it, and it was narcotic and illegal, and it was highly addictive and dangerous. Okay, well, maybe not so much like a cup of coffee. One of my favorite morning rituals became snorting Tylox before getting into the shower. I would get the shower going, line out the Tylox powder on the sink, and snort half in each nostril. Tylox had a distinct burn in my upper nasal passages. It was a good burn—a burn that promised euphoric feelings. In the shower, I would crank up the heat. It felt like the steam speeded up the process. By the time I got out of the shower, I was feeling powerful and reenergized. No longer did I get to pick and choose my using days though. It had to be every day. I couldn't even feel "normal" if I didn't use some kind of narcotics. Working second shifts, it was easier to use during the mornings while my wife was away teaching. Working at a pharmacy, I had anything and everything I wanted.

My first work performance evaluation at ARH was unblemished. I was doing great! My boss, Helen, smiled during my evaluation and made the comment that she was glad to have me on board. I think she used the term *tickled to have me.* This would coincide with my preaddiction phase. When my second evaluation rolled around, things had changed quite dramatically. My work performance was inversely proportional to my drug use. My probationary period was extended another ninety days. Helen wasn't tickled pink anymore. Although she did have a slight reddish tint to her face during that second evaluation. I had been making lots of mistakes: wrong concentrations on suspensions, wrong doses, wrong patient names, and wrong quantities, just to name a few. Once, I dispensed some quinidine, a heart antiarrhythmic medication, instead of quinine, which is used sometimes for leg cramps. I realized it when I went to put the bottle back on the shelf, so I jumped the counter and chased the patient down in her car in the parking lot. I literally had to run up beside the car and flag her down. It's hard to concentrate when your brain is drowning in narcotics.

I had no idea that there was a connection between the mistakes I was making and the drugs I was taking. It never crossed my mind. I just thought I was a bad pharmacist. This depressed me and perpetuated my desire to be numb. I had crossed a line. I had crossed many lines. I was professionally impaired and stealing controlled substances. I was lying to my wife regularly. The formation of two separate lives had begun. My morals, oaths, and vows were all meaningless now. I was in the grip of a progressive and fatal disease, and I didn't even know it.

ACCUSED

As I have mentioned, the ARH clinic pharmacy was my first job as a pharmacist. I had signed a contract with them while in my second year of pharmacy school that paid my tuition in exchange for enslaving myself to them for a term of three years after graduation. My family had no money to help me with tuition, so it was either this or take out more loans. My preceptor and good friend, John Chaney, had paid for my tuition for the first two years out of his pocket. I didn't want him to have to continue to do this. Or perhaps, I just thought it was cool to be able to go to school and brag that I had already signed a contract for a job with a hospital.

I worked the evening shift. The folks that I had signed the contract with had worked very hard to keep me located in Hazard since there were several other locations in not-so-appealing necks of the woods. Not that Hazard was so wonderful, but it was a metropolis compared to some of the other locations that were potential spots for me.

Each day, I came in at two, took a lunch from four to five during which I usually snorted pills, then I worked until we closed at eleven. I had been there about eight months when all hell broke loose.

It was early February, and I worked my usual shift, filling forty or fifty prescriptions from the Prime Time Clinic down the hall. At about ten thirty, my tech asked if she could leave a little early to go hang out with some friends at the North Fork Grill, which was a bar downtown. It wasn't a particularly unusual request. It had been a fairly slow night, so I told her to go ahead. I set the alarm, locked up, and went home right at eleven, perhaps a few minutes after. When I got home, I spent some adult time with Darcey. After she went to bed, I headed next door to my friend Curtis's house to watch a movie and drink some beer. We had rented *The Birdcage*. Curtis had lupus and diabetes and was quite sick most of the time. He was in chronic pain and had great difficulty sleeping. He was always game for a late-night movie and a couple beers. It was something we did fairly often. As usual, we ended up talking all night and throwing some darts, paying no attention to the movie. Some time around 2:00 a.m., and several beers later, I went home and went to bed.

The next morning, I was awakened by the phone ringing. It was my boss, Helen. She informed me that the pharmacy had been burglarized during the night and that I would need to make a statement to the police. No problem I told her, I could do that. She said that a large amount of drugs had been taken.

I got up, grabbed some stale coffee that Darcey had made around six, and crushed up a couple Lortab while waiting for the microwave to heat the coffee. A marble mortar and pestle I had received as a graduation gift had come in handy for crushing pills. I enjoyed my narcotic breakfast right off the kitchen counter.

I mentally revisited the wake-up call. Helen had said I would need to make a statement to the police. I realized with only abbreviated fear that I would be talking to the police with narcotics in my system. Doing without wasn't an option, but I planned to take it easy. They probably only wanted to ask me if I had seen anything suspicious the night before and that wouldn't take long. There was no reason to get all nervous.

An hour or so later, I was hanging out on the front porch enjoying a crisp, sunny morning when a city police car started down the driveway. The dogs next door began their incessant yowling as they did most of the time. They didn't necessarily need anything to be barking *at*, but a car was always a good excuse. Sometimes at night and into the early hours of the morning, those dogs would bark at absolutely nothing. Mama dog would have a litter of pups and then eventually breed with one of the male pups, creating a bunch of inbred mutts. One in particular, I would frequently see standing on its owner's deck, barking into the night sky. I've stood out there before and watched, just to see if maybe there was something that I had missed, like a cat or a drunken neighbor stumbling home, or perhaps an asteroid shooting across the sky, but there wasn't. It just wanted to sound its obnoxious, whining, ceaseless, inbred howl into the air. Many nights I was awakened by this and sometimes stayed awake, imagining what I would like to do to this retarded animal. One night in particular, I had lain in bed listening to the dog howl at nothing. It had awakened me at about two in the morning. I found myself rifling through the house for something to throw at it. I didn't want to kill it, and I didn't want to make a loud noise or damage my neighbor's house, but I wanted to hurt it. In the kitchen pantry, I found my ammunition. A large sack of potatoes was my arsenal. I grabbed a handful and walked outside on my porch. It was cold but dry, and my quarry stood there, howling into the night sky at absolutely nothing. As a baseball player in grade school and part of high school, I never was really known for my throwing accuracy, but I had plenty of potatoes and a deep resentment. Standing in my underwear, I wound up and launched the first potato torpedo. It was a miss, and Brownie, a solid black dog, continued bellowing. Somewhere around the third or fourth grenade, I hit pay dirt. A medium-sized potato thrown from a distance of thirty to thirty-five yards hit the animal on the rump, generating a delightful and gratifying squeal from Brownie the black dog. She ran squalling underneath the deck, and a glorious silence ensued. I had won the *battle of retarded dog*.

The police car was driven by Russell Dishner, a guy who was a couple years younger than me whom I had gone to school and church with all my life. He was a Hazard City police officer now. He said I needed to go down to the police station to make a statement, and that I could just follow him down there. I put on my clothes, snorted one more line of Lortab, and drove to the station behind Russell. I had no idea that I was actually a suspect in the burglary, or that I was walking into a seriously heated interrogation.

The officers at the station guided me into an interrogation room with a table, chairs, two-way mirror—the whole *Law and Order* getup. I sat down across from a cop I knew named Gary. He was married to one of the day-shift pharmacists that I worked with. Coincidentally, he had at one point suggested that I was fooling around with his wife, Lisa. I was not. When I had just started my job at the clinic, I naturally had many questions in the evenings when by myself. I would call his wife,

Lisa, at home to ask her questions. This was the basis for his accusation per Lisa. So it looked like a disaster waiting to happen. It's never good when a cop thinks you're fooling around with his wife.

After I sat down, he started with the Miranda rights. I felt the blood drain from my head, and I almost passed out. My stomach twisted into a knot, and I got violently nauseous.

"Am I a suspect?" I gasped.

"There was no sign of forced entry, and you were the last one leaving the pharmacy," he replied. "We'll be questioning everybody that has a key to the pharmacy, but we're starting with you."

He began asking me the basic questions about the previous night. What time did I leave? Where did I go after I left? Did anybody see me leave? Then the good cop-bad cop routine began. The other officer came busting in the door, holding a VHS tape over his head screaming that he *knew* I had taken all the drugs, and it was all on this tape he had in his hand. There was a quarter of a million dollars street value of various controlled substances stolen, and he had *me* on tape taking them. I suggested that there might be some *Bugs Bunny* episodes on his tape, but there most definitely was *not* any footage of me taking *any* drugs from *any* pharmacy. Quite a goofy thing to say, I admit now. It was the best I could come up with under the stressful conditions. He insisted that I was on the tape. I insisted that I was not. Still, under these circumstances, I was petrified. This was very serious stuff, and they were not kidding. These were real cops, and this was an actual interrogation.

Gary, oddly playing the role of good cop, would try to settle the other one down. I would have thought Gary to be the one assigned to bad cop due to the aforementioned accusations. He told his partner that I was cooperating and that he should calm down a bit and perhaps give me a chance to talk. Perhaps, I needed a glass of water or a soda. Then he insisted that he was only there to *help* me. If I had something to say, I needed to be honest and say it now. He assured me that the mildest of penalties would apply if I simply told them what happened. Back and forth we went. At one point, they both left the room, and I was in the room by myself. I could feel them observing me through the mirror. When they came back, they strongly suggested once again that if I had *anything* to tell them, now was the time. They would go as easy on me as possible if I confessed. I told them I had nothing to confess, so they let me leave with the promise that I would be hearing from them soon.

As I stood to leave, a wave of emotions overwhelmed my brain. *How could this be happening to me? Why did they give me such a hard time? What was going to happen?* I needed to vomit. I could feel acid building in my stomach and slight cramping. My saliva glands went into overdrive, and my breathing was shallow and fast.

By the time I walked out the front door of the police station, I was in shock. I couldn't believe that I was a suspect. I walked across the street to city hall where my mom worked and told her what had happened. I broke down crying as I told her. More nausea. More hyperventilating. More dizziness. She hugged me and assured me that it would be okay.

Next, I drove down to the pharmacy to talk to my boss.

"You don't think I did this, do you? You don't believe this crap the police are suggesting, do you?" I asked.

"Well, I don't know what to think. I'm just going to let the police do their job," she replied.

To me, this meant that she thought it was me. She did. I felt like all my coworkers were looking at me strangely. They were.

The police questioned everybody and asked us all to take polygraphs. This would pose an immediate problem for me since I was stealing and using narcotics from my employer. I didn't know much about polygraphs at the time, and I didn't know what to do. I asked some friends and acquaintances what they thought and also scoured the Internet for answers. The advice I got was unanimous. The polygraph was an *interrogation tool* used to scare people. The main purpose is to get a guilty person very nervous so that they confess. It also helps by pointing investigators in a direction when somebody refuses. Unfortunately for me, I needed to decline.

Polygraphs work by detecting your body's reactions—like respiratory rate, heart rate, sweating of fingertips, and blood pressure—as you are asked certain questions. They are only advantageous to the police and will not help you in any way. There is just too much room for nervousness to be misconstrued as a positive for a lying reaction. I was quite nervous as one can imagine. I was so nervous that I ended up telling them I wouldn't be volunteering for their polygraph. As it turned out, I was the only one that declined to take one, probably because I was the only one stealing drugs and snorting them in the bathroom each night. That might as well have been a confession to them. This was made obvious as the investigation seemed to focus more and more in my direction as days passed. All other avenues were ignored from that day forth.

The biggest reason that I didn't like the idea of taking a polygraph was obviously the fact that I had been taking drugs from the pharmacy for months. My addiction had grown from a pill here and there to daily use and dependence. Over the course of several months, I had taken more than a few. I was high every evening at work. I was afraid that they would ask me questions that would get me fired if I answered them honestly yet make me look like a liar if I didn't. Such is the life of a lying, stealing, and addicted pharmacist.

I began reading more about the polygraph machines. The more I read, the more I questioned why these things were even allowed to be used in any situation. I ran across an article called "How to Sting the Polygraph." The author, Doug Williams, is a certified police polygraph expert. He had worked for the Oklahoma City police for about ten years and ran thousands of polygraphs. He claimed to be able to teach anybody to pass a polygraph no matter what the situation. Being truthful or not, nervous or not, Doug said his technique would teach a person to pass. I downloaded the article. If ever I was going to have to take one of these, I was going to at least understand what was going on and be well prepared. This would later be used against me in the prosecution's discovery after they pulled it from my computer at home.

For several days, detectives showed up at the pharmacy and individually took us in the breakroom to further question us. Within a few days, the investigation was taken over by the FBI and Kentucky State Police. Move over Barney. The big dogs were cutting in.

They continued to question, and I continued to tell them that I had done nothing. Unbeknownst to me, the FBI had installed hidden cameras in various locations throughout the pharmacy.

After several police questioning ambushes at the pharmacy, I eventually decided out of fear to talk to an attorney. I told no one that I was doing this, but by the next day, the cops knew. A comment was made as to why I was "lawyering up" if I wasn't hiding something.

I was referred to an attorney named Danny Rose. He was a local defense attorney. I told him what had happened, and he advised me that the next time they wanted to question me, they would have to contact him. He also strongly advised me that I shouldn't take *so much as an aspirin* from the pharmacy.

A week or so later, I was at work at the pharmacy, when my attorney called me. He said several FBI agents and a U.S. attorney had just left his office, making all kinds of threats. He said I needed to come down there to his office immediately to talk. My heart sank, my stomach knotted, and I was dizzy. I hung up the phone in tears and told Sherri, another pharmacist who was my immediate supervisor, I needed to leave and I probably wouldn't make it back for the rest of my shift. I didn't wait for her reply. I just left in a frenzy of fear and dread.

It was a long drive to Danny Rose's office that day. I cried and prayed out loud the whole way. *Please, God, don't let this be bad. Please, God, don't let this be bad. Please help me, God, please.* When I got there, Danny seemed a little shaken himself. I don't know if he had ever had a visit like that from a group of threatening feds. He implored me to talk to him if I had *anything* that I needed to say. He was on my side and wanted to be able to help me to the best of his abilities. In order to do this, he needed to know everything. Once again, I told him there was nothing to tell. The feds had, of course, promised to go nice and easy on me if I would confess. Again, I told him I had nothing to confess. I had to assure him of this several times before he would make the call to them and tell them I had nothing. They assured me that if I insisted on not talking, they would indict me within ten days.

Ten days came and went without hearing from them. It was a terrifying ten days. The bullies had been bluffing.

During my next meeting with Danny, he suggested that I retain another attorney. He had never argued a case in federal court, and he didn't want to experiment with my freedom on the line if it indeed came down to that. He recommended Ned Pillersdorf. Like the Smucker's Jelly commercial, I figured with a name like Pillersdorf, he *had* to be good. Ned was a seasoned federal court criminal defense lawyer located in Prestonsburg. Many of the federal cases in the area wound up on Ned's desk because he was good. He wasn't cheap though. A five-thousand-dollar retainer was required, and I had to start borrowing money. My mother-in-law loaned me five grand, and my father-in-law another five.

During my first visit with Ned, I gave him my story. He agreed to take on the case. We both agreed that it would be best to continue not hearing from the prosecutors or investigators at all, but we would get ready for them just in case.

Ned's office was a mess. There were stacks of paperwork and manila folders all over his desk and pretty much any surface in the office, including the floor and file cabinets. He was a nerdy-looking man with glasses, a thick mustache, and two tufts of hair on either side of his head. He had an air of confidence about him that comforted me. As I described the situation to him that had brought me to his office, he gave me a boost of confidence by shaking his head at the lack of any possible case they could ever present against me. It was preposterous what the feds could get by. They had no case! He would bury them!

I told him about the polygraph, and he applauded me for refusing to take it. He gave me a thirty-minute lecture on how misleading polygraphs were and how nobody should *ever* agree to take them. He was passionate about this. He had statistics to back up his stance.

"If you never learn anything else from me, Jared, learn that police-directed polygraphs are only tools to help the police and *never* the accused," he told me. "They're nothing but bullying tools."

If they wanted a polygraph though, we *could* give them one, if I was sure that I could pass it. I was. He knew a gentleman in West Virginia that was an independent polygrapher. He used to work for the police department for years but had retired and offered his services now for a fee of five hundred dollars. I could schedule a session with him, and he would run a polygraph on me. We would submit these results to the investigators and perhaps convince them that they should look elsewhere. It sounded good to me. Ned set up the appointment.

I embarked for Huntington to meet the polygrapher. I was anxious. I premedicated with beta blockers and a touch of Xanax to make the test go as smoothly as possible. Beta blockers block the receptors that are responsible for your *fight-or-flight* responses. They would help me appear as calm as possible by limiting my heart rate and dulling any tremor.

When I got to his office, he propped his feet up on his desk and asked me to tell him about the situation that got me there. From this, he would devise a series of questions to ask me. He then proceeded to hook me up to an ensemble of wires and gadgets that would supposedly tell if I was speaking the truth or not.

He then began asking me questions, which, I had already learned, were *control* questions. These were questions that were asked with the specific intention of eliciting a positive response with which they could compare any future positive responses. Questions like, "Have you ever taken something from work that you weren't supposed to?" and "Have you ever thought about cheating on your spouse?" The predicted *uneasy* response will give a spike on the polygraph that is compared to spikes made by asking relevant questions later in the test. While you're sitting there, thinking, *Hmmm, well, I have taken a pen from work before and technically it wasn't mine,* your body is producing a reaction recorded by the machine.

After these came the relevant questions. I made sure in the pretest interview that he would stick to the questions relevant to the specific occurrence for which I was being investigated. I was asked if I took the drugs from the pharmacy that went missing on the specific night in question. I was asked if I knew who took them. I was asked if I was lying.

At the end of the exam, I asked him what his test results concluded. He said that according to the polygraph, I was telling the truth. He said, "I would let you know real quickly if you were lying to me 'cause I don't like liars."

I was given a copy of the results, and then I was on my way. I took the results to my attorney, who forwarded the results to the prosecutor and his demons.

Weeks and months went by with no harassment from cops or prosecutors. All white Grand Marquis cars I feared were following me though. Any vans that drove through my neighborhood, I was sure they were loaded down with FBI guys and electronic surveillance equipment. All cops were surely watching me. I was constantly looking over my shoulder and in my rearview mirror. It was a torturous and unsettling life. I remember running into my first attorney, Danny Rose, at Wal-Mart one evening in the early summer. He asked me what was going on. I told him I hadn't heard anything, and we agreed that this was good news. We assumed that they had moved on to another suspect. We were wrong.

As can be predicted, I didn't keep my nose clean very long. Once the heat started to dwindle, I began using heavily again. I didn't know that my every move was being watched at work. Every morning following my shift the night before, the supervising pharmacists were required to inventory all controlled substances. Four or five hidden cameras had been installed in various places throughout the pharmacy, and they were documenting everything. I got lazy again and predictably careless. The FBI gave me a little bit of rope with which to hang myself, and I tied the noose securely around my neck.

THE RIGHT TO REMAIN SILENT

On Friday, August 25, 1997, I came in to work. It wasn't my normal day to work, but I had been called in to cover a shift. I find it quite ironic now because I was actually thinking to myself on my way to work how I was *so* glad that the whole investigation thing had blown over and gone away. I had spent several months looking over my shoulder and worrying that at any moment, a cop was going to come charging in the pharmacy asking more questions or worse. For several months prior, every time I saw a car that looked like an undercover, I knew without a doubt that they were following me. There had been phone taps on my home phone, I was pretty sure. Those guys had found out that I had hired a lawyer before I told anybody. That's a fact. But things had now gone quiet. There had been no more blitzkrieg questioning or unannounced appearances by them at the pharmacy. Things had seemed to be getting back to *normal.* I was back to regular using again on a daily basis. Finally, I thought as I pulled into the parking lot, they had given up and left me alone. I was very, very wrong.

I showed up around 9:00 a.m. to cover a shift for Lisa, who, I was told, had called in sick. I came in the back door of the clinic building as I always did and bumped into Lisa. "I thought you were sick."

"Oh, uh, yeah. I, uh, am going to the clinic . . . to the doctor. Then I'm going home," she replied nervously. Although this puzzled me briefly, I shrugged it off. Lisa was a nervous-type person on any given day, so it wasn't entirely strange. She was a very sweet and likable person, but her husband was controlling, oppressive, and apparently an alcoholic, according to her. She was reflexively meek, apologetic, and anxious most of the time. I suspected nothing and walked on in through the back door of the pharmacy, and into the trap.

I had just finished swallowing a handful of Ultram to help make the day tolerable when I looked up and saw some police officers being let in the side door of the pharmacy work area. This door was usually used to let the guy in who delivered our drug order. That way, he could roll his dolly in with all the totes on it. Nobody else came in that door. My heart jumped to my throat, and panic surrounded me. They came straight for me and began reading me the Miranda rights. I had the right to remain silent. Anything I said could and would be used in court against me. My knees buckled, and they caught me and placed me in handcuffs. I had the right to an attorney. If I could not afford one, then some completely useless loser would be provided to me at no cost. I went numb. I was confused. I was terrified.

While this was going on at work, my home was being raided by a ridiculous number of police officers, as if I were a suspected terrorist. My dog, Baxter, ferociously threatened to bite them. Good boy, Baxter. They turned my house upside down, looking for potential evidence. Pictures were thrown about. Clothes were taken out of closets, strewn about, and not put back. Drawers were opened, ransacked, and left open. My computer was accessed, and many things were printed, including the article on polygraphs. Letters from me to Darcey were confiscated. My poor wife didn't know what to do. She called work to find out what was going on and was told that I had been arrested.

As they led me out the front door, a skinny red-headed guy from the local TV station with a camera on his shoulder was filming my arrest for the local news. The camera weighed more than he did. He resembled an ant carrying a whole chocolate chip cookie. I wanted to kick him. I thought about unleashing a fierce kick to his chest because I hated him being all up in my face with his camera. He was the icing on this humiliating and horrifying cake. In the parking lot, my Honda Passport was being carefully combed over by still more police. I'm gonna put the police count at around fifteen at this point. I guess there wasn't much else going on that afternoon that required police presence. They put me in the police car and took me to the state police post where I was fingerprinted and processed. Then I was quickly on my way to Ashland, Kentucky, in the back of an unmarked police car where a federal magistrate awaited me to decide if indictment would be pursued.

I don't remember the drive well or much about arriving at the court. I do recall staring out the window as we drove down Highway 80, feeling scared, alone, and anesthetized. Then on to Highway 25 north. I recall the high smokestacks as we passed the oil refineries in Ashland. I had no idea what was going on. I didn't understand the process that was manipulating my life. They tried to explain things to me, but I didn't understand between the shock and the Ultram. The officers were pleasant and left me alone for the most part. I sat in the backseat and cried and stared out the window, contemplating my situation. I cried until my head hurt, and my tear ducts ran dry.

I cannot face prison. I cannot be away from my family. This is where I initially began to seriously entertain the thought of suicide. What's the best way to go? I remembered reading about a cult a few months earlier called Heaven's Gate. Thirty-eight people that thought a spaceship, which was hiding behind the comet Hale-Bop, would pick up their souls as it flew by the earth if they committed suicide at a particular time. They took their own lives by ingesting phenobarbital and drinking vodka, which together produce a synergistic depressant effect on the central nervous system. This essentially slows the person's breathing down to zero after they are lulled into a nice coma. That sounded like the way to go for me—nice, easy, quiet, peaceful, and without a big mess for family to have to clean up. Maybe I'd throw in some Xanax for good measure.

The court appearance was just another stop in the circus act. The decisions had all been made. The hearing was just a formality. Brief statements were made from the prosecution and my attorney. I had no chance to speak at all.

After my brief appearance in court, I was taken by federal marshals to the Boyd County Detention Center in Catlettsburg, Kentucky. I was checked in and taken to a solitary cell. I overheard the marshals telling them to put me in solitary because I would be safer there. I'm still not sure what they meant by that. Perhaps I looked a little too white-collar for general population. Maybe they weren't ready to let Bubba have his way with me yet. In retrospect, I think it was a strategy to get me to go slightly insane so that I would talk. It definitely challenged any sanity that I might have had, but there was nothing to talk about.

The cell was a five-by-eight concrete-block room with a small metal-frame bed and a stainless steel commode-sink combination. The sink had hot—and cold-water buttons, and it drained into the toilet below. The lighting was a dim fluorescent that went a bit dimmer at some bedtime hour each night. On the bed, which was attached to the wall, was a blue pad about an inch thick which was cracked and stained. There was a sheet and a thin cotton blanket for the bed. The temperature was always cold in the cell. I was wearing polyester orange pants and V-neck shirt with a white T-shirt underneath. I had no underwear on. The guards would not let me wear the ones I had been wearing because they were not white. Apparently, grey underwear is contraband in their jail. Let me tell you, a man in a cold jail cell with polyester pants rubbing against his penis is in for some uncomfortable friction.

The door had a window, which was covered up by a small trapdoor on the outside so that guards could peer in periodically to make sure I hadn't hanged myself with a blanket or drowned myself in the commode. Both of these things I briefly considered. There was also a slot where a food tray could be slid through although a lady rolled the cart into my cell each mealtime instead of using that. Right outside my door was a shower, which flowed to a drain in the concrete floor. Beside me was another solitary cell I assume was identical to mine.

I tried to lie down, but my heart raced uncontrollably. It felt like it was beating up in my throat. I wanted to sleep. I wanted to be unconscious. Oh God, what I wouldn't give for some alcohol. For a fifth of bourbon or and handful of Xanax, I would sell my soul. I wanted to shut off my brain. I knew that there was absolutely nothing that I could do to change anything at that moment. My brain was a pinball machine with metal balls bouncing off the sides of my skull. I cried intensely. Again, the thoughts of suicide drifted into my mind. I just wanted to shut off my brain! I wanted the feelings of panic and fear to stop! Worst-case scenarios flooded my brain. Prison bars and loneliness and jail food and Bubba-the-cellmate taunted me. In-jail visitations from my wife would eventually dwindle to nothing. The kids would be grown when I got out. Eventually, I would tell Darcey just to stay the hell away, divorce me, and get on with life. I wanted to die. I would die. I would kill myself. That's the only way to make this pain stop. I sat on the edge of my metal bed, sobbing and wanting to be dead or at least inebriated by some of my old friends like alcohol or Xanax.

I was cold. I soon learned that to stay warm, I could sit on the toilet bowl with my blanket around me while running hot water. The water would drain into the toilet bowl and heat up the stainless steel, eventually giving me some warmth. When I could make myself, I would sleep. I would awaken from sleeping in a cold, terrified sweat, which would cause me to be cold again. My heart would be back up in my throat, beating so hard I could hear it in my ears. I could rarely sleep more than an hour or two at a time. Each time I awoke, the cold hard truth hit me that this was *not* a dream. Each time I was on the verge of waking up, I would feel that little hint of wishful thinking that it wasn't real. For a fraction of a second before opening my eyes to the concrete-block cell, I could almost convince myself that it *was* just a dream. Then the walls, the stainless steel commode, and the locked steel door all rudely reminded me where I was. I was not going to finally wake up in my king-sized bed at home with Baxter lying beside me.

It was impossible to know what time of day it was with no clocks or outside windows. I just cried, panicked, slept, paced, and prayed. I felt like I knew how those poor Siamese fighting fish feel when they are confined to those tiny softball-sized fishbowls.

Before leaving the courthouse, I had learned that I would be in jail until Tuesday. I would have a detention hearing then which would decide how much my bond would be if I were to be released. Five days and four nights I would be spending in this hell with only myself to talk to and only my insane thoughts to think. There was no hope in my cell. Desperation, suicide, hopelessness, fear, and panic were my only visitors.

To some, five days may not sound like much, but keep in mind that I wasn't sure if I was ever getting out of there or not. The sentencing guidelines on my charges carried lengthy prison terms from ten to twenty years. My attorney gave me a statistic that 83 percent of all federal cases were won by the feds. That meant I had a 17 percent chance of being found not guilty if I went to trial. I didn't like those odds. I was absolutely terrified and had decided that there was no way that I could spend twenty years in prison. If I ended up getting such a sentence, I would kill myself like the Heaven's Gate people did. A handful of phenobarbital followed by a bottle of vodka would allow me to float out of this world. I couldn't handle the thought of being separated from my family for that length of time. I knew that I shouldn't mention any of this to anybody because it would decrease my chances of getting out on Tuesday if such talk was known. Since I was the only one in the cell, I told nobody. Later, when I was released, I actually procured the bottle of phenobarbital tablets that I intended to use if necessary. Hopeless, distraught, terrified, angry, desolate, and sad, I prayed for help over and over. I prayed for relief from the pain. I prayed for freedom. I prayed specifically to get to go home on Tuesday after the detention hearing.

As mentioned before, pacing around the cell in circles was my way of passing time. I paced and cried and paced and cried. Around and around in stupid insane circles in my tiny cell, I exercised to fatigue my muscles and run from the terror. Pacing, crying, and praying . . . pacing, crying, and praying . . . pacing, crying, and praying. All the while entertaining suicide, a permanent solution to a temporary problem.

There was a paperback book in the cell. It was a murder novel, which I ended up reading twice over the weekend. I continued to be cold most of the time. Once daily, I was allowed out of my cell to take a shower for about eight or ten minutes. It was lukewarm water, but it was wonderful. It was the highlight of my day. I stood there underneath the stream, trying to soak in as much of the heat as possible. I leaned my head forward against the block wall and enjoyed the mild warmth. I wished it would get hotter, but it wouldn't. Apparently, decently hot water was voted out when nonwhite underwear was. I didn't have any antiperspirant deodorant to put on after the shower, and I had to put the same clothes back on, so I was still quite pungent within minutes after showering. Once, they let me go to a different room for an hour or so to watch some TV. It was cold in there too. It was still nice though, to get a change of scenery and because *The Andy Griffith Show* was on, and I love that show. It was slightly comforting, like a thimble of water in a hot, dry dessert.

The meals they brought me were beyond bad. I can remember eating applesauce and drinking milk, but not really touching any of the other alleged food. Mashed potatoes served to me one day appeared to be an emulsion of sawdust and milk. I ate what I could, but depression stole my appetite. What I wanted was a nice big fat blue line of Xanax to snort away the pain and anxiety. I knew that would help. I knew that from experience. They wouldn't be serving that though. I would have given a thousand dollars for some booze or pills. Anything to dull the pain. I would have offered years off my life for relief.

My family came to visit me one day. It was a gloomy and distressing visit. I was cold and shivering and on the other side of a Plexiglas wall, which broke my mom's heart even more. There was my mom, my dad, Darcey, and my sister, Michelle. They had to take turns speaking into the telephone device. When it came my dad's turn, he just broke down and couldn't even talk to me. It was just too much for him.

My mom insisted that they get a Bible to me, and eventually, they brought me a New Testament with Psalms and Proverbs. She would have taken hostages if they had not met this demand. Scouring the pages for messages of hope in my desperate situation, I found some in God's promises. Faith and trust in God offered a hint of optimism that was real, but difficult to sustain in the confines of my cell and the impending doom of federal court.

It seemed like weeks until Tuesday arrived. I was never really sure what time of day it was. I was finally taken to my hearing by the federal marshals, wearing handcuffs on my wrists and shackles around my legs. Guards led me shuffling into the courtroom. Shuffling both because of the short chain on the shackles and the chaffing caused by the aforementioned absence of underwear aggravated by polyester pants. Some statements were made by the prosecution and some by my defense. The details of which are lost on me, but apparently, some things were said that were unacceptable and unbelievable to my family. My cousin Matt was quickly kicked out of the courtroom for yelling *bullshit* after the prosecution said something he didn't agree with. My dad and my wife were escorted out as well for making sounds of disapproval in the courtroom when certain suggestions were put forth by the prosecution.

Then the judge announced her decision that I could be released on a ten-thousand-dollar surety bond. Basically, my parents could put their house up as the surety. I was overjoyed. I knew that there was still a host of hurdles to jump, but this was a victory in so many ways. I was getting to go home! I could take a bath! I could have sex! I could sleep in a real bed with sheets! I could wear underwear of any color I wanted! I envisioned myself sitting in my whirlpool tub with a cold beer in my hand. I could have a drink! I could have twenty drinks! Oh, it felt so good to know I was going home, to know booze was near. Home, where there would be alcohol and Xanax. Home, where I could talk to my family without a phone and without Plexiglas. Home, where my mom's mashed potatoes would be delicious, and water would be hot, and I could wear grey underwear or blue or red or green. One thing for sure, I would *not* wear orange for a while though. I hated orange now; thanks to the outfit I had worn for the past five days.

By the time that we were done in court, it was after 5:00 p.m. We needed a copy of the house deed, and the courthouse was closed in Hazard. I didn't want to go back to that cell. My family didn't want me to have to either. My mom and my dad made a call to Mrs. Baker that worked at the courthouse. Yes, she would be happy to go back to the courthouse and fax us a copy of that deed so that I could be released. God bless you, Mrs. Baker! Soon the shackles were off, and I was free—for now anyway. The First Baptist Church van awaited us in the parking lot, and we all rode home together with Bro. Ron Sholar at the wheel. Darcey held me, and we cried together in the back.

When I got home, all I wanted to do was drink and take a bath. I felt disgusting. Although I had enjoyed those lukewarm showers at the jail, I wanted to soak in a nice hot whirlpool tub, put on clean clothes, and use some deodorant. But first, I needed some beer! I wanted a beer more than I wanted anything else.

I walked down to the store just down the street to buy a twelve-pack of beer, even before walking into Mom and Dad's house. We didn't go to my house. It was still a wreck from the storm of police officers that searched it on Friday. I couldn't go there for days. It was too depressing. We stayed the next couple of weeks at my parents' house in the guestroom. With my twelve-pack acquired, the drinking had begun. This would be the beginning of a three-month binge that would be the heaviest period of daily drinking of my life.

PRETRIAL ETERNITY

I was released at the end of August, and my case was to be handed to a grand jury in September. I was convinced with the lack of evidence that I would not get indicted. Everything they had was circumstantial, and much of it was downright ridiculous. A friend called me up and offered me his houseboat at Laurel Lake for the weekend. This was the day before the grand jury was to hear my case. He knew I would be anxious, and his boat would be a great way to try to relax while enjoying some Corona. I went over on Thursday by myself, armed with copious amounts of beer. My dad was going to meet me Friday evening. I drank heavily Friday from the moment I woke up. When I got drunk enough and brave enough, I went to a pay phone on the dock and called my mom to get the results of my grand jury hearing. She gave me the bad news I had dreaded hearing. I had indeed been indicted, despite a woeful lack of evidence. My heart sank. Yes, apparently, even a ham sandwich can be indicted as they say. Oh well, I was one step closer to spending a significant portion of my life in prison, and the prospect of suicide gained more serious contemplation. For now, I would drink away the fear. Again, my best friend alcohol would lift me to an existence of life that was slightly tolerable. I drank as hard as I could drink. Oblivion, here I come.

My trial date was scheduled for December 3rd. I was jobless, depressed, and I was drinking vodka profusely. We finally moved back into our own house after a couple of weeks. Darcey was still teaching at the grade school, but her income was not enough to sustain us. Bill collectors began to call. I was behind on my student loan payments, my car lease, and all credit cards. The car leasing company threatened me. I told them to come get the Honda Passport that was sitting at the state police post. The credit card companies called. I told *them* to go to hell.

I began washing cars to make some money. This was humiliating. Everybody in town knew about my arrest, and I had to crawl up to these people and ask them if I could wash their car. More than anything else, I wanted money to buy booze with since I knew my family wouldn't give me cash for this. They knew exactly what I wanted it for. I went to businesses and to people that I knew, offering to detail their cars. Some days I would make some good cash. Other days I would make barely thirty dollars. All days, I lied to Darcey about how much I made so that I could buy plenty of vodka. That was my priority.

On a couple occasions, I sneaked a day of work at a pharmacy out of town. The owners and managers of which didn't know about my legal situation. I needed the money desperately. I prayed that the board didn't find out since I had been required to sign an agreed order a few days after the arrest that required me to let the board know anytime I was going to work as a pharmacist. An enormous and unfeasible amount of paperwork and preparation was ordered to take place at any location I was to work, so I simply disregarded the order. It was on these occasions that I procured the phenobarbital which I planned to use to kill myself if I so decided.

Vodka had become my best friend in the whole world. When I would wake up each morning while Darcey was at her teaching job, I would try desperately to go back to the more peaceful land of sleep. When it became evident that I couldn't, I would immediately reach for my vodka bottle. The fear, panic, and dread overtook me from the moment I woke up. My heart would race uncontrollably, and every morning, I would awaken in a cold sweat with my heart up in my throat again and my hair wet from the tossing and turning and nightmares throughout the night. My throat would be tight. I would talk to myself out loud, saying things like, "Oh God, I can't believe this is happening. Oh God, I can't believe this is my life. Oh God, I just want to die."

My dog, Baxter, is the greatest dog in the whole world, paws down. We got him in 1995 from the animal shelter here in Lexington, Kentucky. Every day when I would wake up to the horror of my life, he would be right there beside me, ready to console me in any way he could. He knew that something was wrong, and he tried to lick the problem away. He would lie down beside me and lick my face to try to make things better. Occasionally, it would make me smile. He wouldn't leave my side. He can't stand the sight of tears. If he sees them, they *must be licked away.* He feels it is his duty. If he notices a tone in your voice that depicts anger or sadness, he gets concerned. He will get up and walk over to you to see if he needs to intervene with some licking therapy or rapid tail wagging. If there is not a heaven for dogs, I bet Baxter shows up in human heaven.

After consuming a half-pint of vodka for breakfast, the outlook no longer looked so dim. The evidence was weak, I had a good lawyer, God was on my side, and the world was a fair place! I could actually talk about it once the vodka kicked in. I felt better, and Baxter felt better. I could hold my head up. I could smile.

My family begged me not to drink. I told them that *not drinking* was *not* an option, and they had might as well lay off. I think they knew that I was determined to drink. I hid it as much as I could, but everybody knew what was in the cups I carried everywhere. I explained that without alcohol, I couldn't function. I promised that once I got through this hell, I would slow down, but for now, this was the only way I could bear the pain of my life.

Some days, my stomach would hurt severely. I knew that the vodka was probably doing some physical harm to my stomach lining. I didn't care. If I lived through it, I would deal with that later. If I had eaten any lunch or dinner, I would usually make myself throw up so that nothing impeded the absorption of the alcohol. I threw up often. One morning, my stomach revolted on me. I drank my usual first dose of vodka mixed in some water. When it came back up, I directed it right back into the glass that I had used to drink it. On a very tight alcohol budget, I was forced to recycle. On the count of three, with a chaser of milk, I drank down the vodka, water, stomach acids, and whatever that little red floating thing was. I gritted my teeth and strained until I had successfully held it down. Once again, I was armed with liquid courage to face the day. Grimace if you will, but that's no worse than that *Man vs. Wild* show where a guy was holding an elephant turd above his head and squeezing water from it into his mouth! He did it! I saw it!

I hated the mailbox. It was my enemy. It seemed like each week brought more bad news. Ominous envelopes with pages inside reading *The United States of America v. Jared Combs* or some document outlining my charges and the sentencing guidelines. Or perhaps they had found something brand new to charge me with. Ten to twenty years bounced around inside my head like a pinball in a pinball machine. It was always some kind of bad news in the form of prosecutors or bill collectors. Sometimes I would wait days before collecting the mail.

I walked next door one day shortly after my release to talk to my friend Curtis. I began explaining to him what had happened, pleading my case to him and fearing his judgment. He stopped me in midsentence.

"I don't care what you did or didn't do. You are my friend, Jared, and I'm here for ya." Those words stick with me today. He was a true friend. Curtis died of heart failure related to a long battle with lupus and diabetes just a few years later in his early thirties.

For the three months prior to my trial, I continued to drink incessantly. Every day, I welcomed my liquid courage. For trips to see my lawyer in Prestonsburg, my dad usually drove me, both for support and probably because my family knew I would be intoxicated and, therefore, dangerous behind the wheel of a car.

One day my attorney, Ned, called me and said that the television station was interested in interviewing us to tell my side of the story. Ned thought it would be a good idea since I had been on the news being arrested and indicted. Any member of a potential jury would have seen the negative news. I agreed, and we met at his office for the interview. During the interview, I explained that I was no pharmacy burglar and that the feds had the wrong guy.

In effort to stop the prosecutor from sending me to prison for twenty years, I asked Ned if I could admit to the one charge of *obtaining a controlled substance by deception.* I had indeed taken some pills for my personal use. They had video of me doing this, and I was willing to admit my use and take that responsibility. That wouldn't be possible, according to Ned. Somehow, the sentencing guidelines were all linked together. If I pled to the one charge, the feds could use the sentencing guidelines for all the charges in the indictment combined. I could still be faced with ten to twenty years even though the guidelines for the charge of *obtaining a controlled substance by deception* were only one to five years. I didn't really understand it, but I figured he knew what he was talking about.

Scared, embarrassed, and ashamed, I stayed home as much as possible. My life was on hold. I had a loving supportive family and, of course, my vodka; but I still felt alone. Occasionally, my vodka would offer me a glimmer of hope and a promise of freedom. Between my family, prayer, Baxter, and the vodka, I managed to somehow not commit suicide although I would think about it almost daily. Some days, I would open the bottle of phenobarb tablets and ponder this solution, albeit a bad one.

At night, I would cry to Darcey, and she would hold me and assure me that God would take care of us. I prayed that he would. I just didn't think that he cared about *me* anymore. I had done some bad things, and I had run from Him for the last several years. I had been a self-will run riot. My own selfish wants and desires are all I had pursued, ignoring God. Now I came begging for His help. I pictured God looking down upon me with disdain and turning his face away.

THE TRIAL BEGINS (AND ENDS)

December finally came. We drove over to the federal courthouse in Pikeville for jury selection. I was, of course, wearing a coat and tie and trying to appear composed. I had my usual vodka for breakfast and stowed the rest in my coat pocket in the van. We examined the list of potential jurors and made some decisions on some to strike and some to keep. Striking anybody that might have any law enforcement connections and keeping anybody that might be somewhat sympathetic, we picked our jury. It was a circus.

The prosecution quickly offered me a deal. They would arrange zero jail time if I cooperated. All I had to do was "admit my involvement" in the burglary. They could make no promises as to what actions the board of pharmacy might take, but they *could* take prison time, my greatest fear, off the table.

"I can't do that," I told Ned. "I can't admit to something I didn't do."

"I didn't think so," he replied. "They offered so I had to run it by you."

The promise of no jail time was, however, tempting. I wouldn't have to be away from my family. I wouldn't have to be faced with the possibility of being confined to a prison cell by battling the feds and their conviction rate of 83 percent. Bubba wouldn't have the chance to get me as a roommate to play with. *So what* if I would never practice pharmacy again. I could do something else. I would figure that out later. Guaranteed freedom was tempting.

"Should I make up a story to give them so I can take them up on this?"

"No, Jared. We can't do that. We don't make up stories. We've got a strong case. Let's go to trial," he said confidently.

Sure, Ned. It's not gonna be you ironing Bubba's shirts now, is it? On with the circus!

Then it was time for opening statements. The prosecutor led off with his theory. He looked tired. Probably, I thought, because he had been out all night poisoning puppies or throwing cuddly kittens from bridges. As he paced back and forth in front of us, claiming that I had stolen a truckload of drugs worth a quarter million dollars, I couldn't help but notice how surreal this was. I was really a defendant in a federal case. This wasn't a *Law and Order* episode. My freedom depended on how well this little bald guy with a funny name to my left put on a show. There was a real possibility that I could go to prison. How many times in the past ten months had I wished to wake up from this nightmare to a warm summer morning with my dog, Baxter, at my side? That I would open my eyes and see the sheer curtains being tossed by a warm breeze coming through the open windows, a lawnmower droning in the distance, and the obnoxious inbred dogs barking next door at absolutely nothing? It never happened though. I always woke up to the hateful truth that owned my life.

According to the prosecution, I had stolen practically every controlled substance in the ARH pharmacy's inventory in a time span of about five minutes. I had carefully planned the heist right after a large delivery of narcotics had come in that day. I had somehow gotten this load out to my vehicle unnoticed by anyone. I had then disseminated the drugs through a vast network of unnamed and unidentified dope dealers, or perhaps made a delivery during my visit to Chicago in April, using the John Mellencamp concert as an excuse for traveling there. Yea, that was a great theory. I got on Southwest Airlines with a suitcase full of narcotics. These guys have *no* idea how much I love John Mellencamp obviously! I would *not* have risked missing *that* show!

Nobody saw me take anything; none of the drugs were recovered when they stormed my house and car; and no, Mr. Bad Cop, there *was* no video tape of the crime. Perhaps it *had* been Bugs Bunny after all on that tape.

My attorney batted next. The prosecution's case was completely circumstantial, based solely on the fact that I had been the one that worked the night before. They had no witnesses and no evidence to convict his client. The charges should be dismissed due to lack of evidence.

Later, we all agreed that round 1 belonged to Ned. That night, I went home still terrified. I drank some courage, compliments of Tvarski.

The next day, we made the trip back over to Pikeville for another day of courtroom battle. As soon as I crossed the threshold of the courthouse and through the metal detector, Ned came out of the conference room and signaled for me to come in. When I came into the room, he said these words: "Jared, they're blinking on us." I had no idea what that meant, and my heart went into racing mode. Was that a good thing or a bad thing? What's a blink? Should we blink back?

"What does that mean?" I asked frantically. Before he could reply, there was a knock at the conference room door. I opened the door and it was the prosecutor, whom I had previously referred to as Satan. His real name was Mark Wohlander.

"Can I come in?" Satan asked.

"Sure, whatever, I can't stop you," I replied loathingly.

I hated this man. The mere sight of him revolted me. He represented evil to me. He came in and sat at the table opposite of me and Ned. He and Ned had obviously already had a discussion. The words that came next out of his mouth will be etched in my brain forever. It was news that only my God in heaven could have orchestrated and delivered to me in such a time of need.

The prosecutor said, "Jared, I have serious doubts about your guilt, and I can no longer ethically pursue this." Those were his exact words, plus or minus a preposition or so.

I stared at him, not quite able to wrap my brain around what he had just said. Time stopped. I asked him to repeat it. He did, and then he added, "Now we do have you on tape taking some pills for personal use while in the pharmacy, and you'll have to work with me on that, but I'll work that out so that you can get probation." My brain oscillated between jubilance, anger, disbelief, and fear at the speed of light. I wanted to cry and scream. I wanted to hug the prosecutor formerly known as Satan. I wanted to drink. *Does this mean what I think? So that's what a blink is.*

I looked over at Ned to read his reaction as Mr. Wohlander excused himself from the room to allow us to discuss the offer. I was ecstatic, with a slight uneasiness and uncertainty. This was unbelievable! I kept expecting him to slither back in the door and say, "Hah! Gotcha! See you in the courtroom, pharmacy boy!"

My parents came into the room, and Ned explained the offer to them. My mom made some comment about not wanting me to have to plead guilty to a felony at all. Ned said, "Mrs. Combs, this is a win. He'll be going home today instead of facing a trial and possible prison. They are dropping the burglary and possession charges *with prejudice*. I suggest we take the deal."

"Now what does that mean, with prejudice?" I asked.

"Well, it's like this, Jared," Ned answered. "After they drop the charges with prejudice, you can never be tried for it again. If you stand on the top step of the courthouse here in front of a news crew and confess to doing the whole thing, the charges can't be brought on you again."

After a brief discussion with Ned and my family, I told him I would accept the deal. I was going home. Sorry Bubba. Ned was headed, no doubt, to the golf course.

We sat in the conference room and waited for the paperwork to be drawn up and the jury to be dismissed. A short while later, Mr. Wohlander's nice twin who apparently ran the show now, stuck his head in the door to apologize for the delay. It shouldn't be much longer, and he would get us out of there. He actually apologized! It was as if he was a completely different person! His whole demeanor and attitude had changed. The way he looked at me, almost humbly now, contrasted sharply with the previous arrogant attitude he had radiated. I have since had this vision of an angel speaking to him in the middle of the night telling him that he should have a change of heart. I don't know what else to make of it. I do know that there were many prayers said for me and by me. Perhaps this was God's answer. What else could it have been? They had spent hours upon hours investigating me then hours upon hours prosecuting me, and God only knows how much *money* was spent on the ordeal! Then overnight, he completely changed his mind and said he's not going to pursue prosecuting me! You tell me. At what point exactly did he decide he couldn't ethically pursue my prosecution? Was it last night before bed? Was it while he was shaving this morning or during the drive down?

A short while later, I was standing in front of the judge, accepting the terms of my plea bargain. The judge asked me if I completely understood that I was going to be pleading guilty to a felony count of obtaining a controlled substance by deception. I said I did. He asked me if I understood that I would be relinquishing my civil rights such as the right to vote, have a gun, etc., and I said I did. What I really understood was that I was not going to prison for twenty years, and that I wasn't gonna have a roommate named Bubba that liked my perdy mouth, and that I wasn't going to have to kill myself any time soon, and that I would be drinking to my heart's content tonight at home in Hazard.

I walked out of the courthouse doors a free man. I still had to come back for my sentencing in March, but I was assured that I would get probation. My family and I were overjoyed! Our nightmare was over. We got in the van to go home. Darcey and I crawled in the back. Immediately, I reached for my pint bottle of vodka.

"What are you doing?" exclaimed Darcey with a look of disgust and furious disbelief.

"I'm celebrating," I answered.

"After everything that has happened and after what God has done for us, is this how you show your thanks?" She was dismayed.

Taking a drink, my silent answer was yes. It made sense to me. I had just been set free. What more reason did I need to drink? What she didn't understand was, no matter what had just happened, no matter how good God had been to me, I *needed* that drink. I had been drinking very heavily for three months, and my body was screaming for alcohol. I wanted it more than food, sex, or air.

We stopped at Pizza Hut before going home. I went to a pay phone and called my friend George in Chicago to tell him the news. He was happy to hear that it was over, and I was going home. He let out a big *yahoo* over the phone. He was at work, but he said that his coworkers knew all about the trial, and they would understand. While I was on the phone with George, my sister, Michelle, bought me a gift in a nearby Hallmark store. It was a large mug, the size you would eat a large bowl of cereal out of. It said I Love You This Big, and had a picture of a person with arms stretched wide. I still have that mug, and I eat large bowls of cereal out of it. It is my little symbol of freedom.

When we finally got back to Hazard, I was ready to do some serious drinking. I had a couple cases of Coors stashed under my mom and dad's deck. Doesn't everybody have some beer stashed under their parents' deck? My cousin Mac works at a landfill just outside of Evansville, Indiana. One day, a truck dumped several hundred cases of Coors beer at the landfill. Companies would dump things if they had gone out of date or had the least little irregularity with them. He picked up a few cases and gave them to my dad and me. They were perfectly fine for my purposes. When my wife saw me grab a beer and pop the top, she went off the deep end. She started yelling at me. The next thing I know, she ripped the lattice from the bottom of the deck, pulled the cases of beer out, and began slinging individual beers into the road below. One beer at a time, she furiously depleted my supply of free beer. She pelted the road with beer cans, and they exploded on the pavement. I recognized that she was in some sort of psychotic state, and so I proceeded up the hill to my own house. I had a couple stashed up there too, and hopefully, I could get those down before she stomped up the path to stop me.

Back to the
Candy Store

The Parable of the Snake

Once upon a time there was a serpent who was badly injured in a fight with another animal. It managed to slither away to safety but would have surely died if a benevolent man had not seen it suffering by the side of the road. The goodly man carefully wrapped the snake up and took it to his house, where he bestowed the kindest and gentlest care on the snake until it was healed and could return to the wild. Just as the man was releasing the serpent back into the grass, the ungrateful snake turned and bit him on the hand.

"What did you do that for?" cried the man, who knew that the bite of this particular snake was usually fatal. "Didn't I take care of you when no one else would?"

The snake shrugged (no small feat for a snake!) and replied to the benevolent—and now doomed—man, "What did you expect? You knew I was a snake when you picked me up."

Christmas was a little financially tight in 1997. I don't remember much about it actually. I do remember that we were all thankful for my freedom and praying that I could find a job. We were all broke from the previous months of my unemployment and legal battle, so any gifts were reserved for kids only. We were so thankful for my good fortune though that it was one of the better Christmas seasons.

I honestly wish that all Christmas celebrations could be more like this one was. There was little to no focus on gifts and money and buying. These days, it seems like that's all we think about—buying a ridiculous amount of gifts, maxing out credit cards, and having so-called Christmas parties where everybody gets drunk, and Jesus is far from the center of attention. For six weeks prior to December 25 each year, I bet you that no less than fifty people will come up and ask me the question, "Are you ready for Christmas?" What am I supposed to say to that? Am I ready to celebrate the birth of Jesus Christ? Well, yes. Have I spent my three thousand dollars on friends and family yet this year? Not yet.

I received an e-mail in December from a friend named Jeff about a potential job in Pikeville. I had done one of my pharmacy school clinical rotations with him at Pikeville Methodist Hospital. It was a super rotation, one of the better ones. He had a friend that owned an independent pharmacy called Economy Drug in Pikeville that was looking for a pharmacist, if I would be willing to travel the seventy-mile trip. I wasn't exactly in high demand at this point, so *yes,* I told him I would be willing to travel a bit.

I called the number Jeff gave me and set up an interview. My brother-in-law, Kerry, drove me over to the pharmacy in Pikeville. I sat down with Mr. CC Cinnamond in his office, which was back behind the pharmacy through the stockroom double doors. I explained my situation to him. I would get somewhat proficient at *explaining my situation* over the next few years. Anyway, to my dismay, he offered me a job that very day. I would have worked for half of what he offered me. I was so happy! I hadn't worked in about five months besides washing a few cars to make vodka money. I needed income badly. I called Darcey from the pay phone outside and told her the news. God was continuing to watch over us and provide. I had forgotten about God, but he hadn't forgotten about me.

Since the leasing company had been so kind as to remove that monthly payment burden from me for the Honda Passport, I had no transportation. I bought an old Ford Tempo from Kerry for about $500. The transmission slipped a bit, and there was no functional air conditioner, but it would get me from point A to point B.

Economy Drug was a fairly busy pharmacy. Like Rite Aid or CVS, they offered lots of products such as gifts, snacks, toiletries, etc. Some days, we would fill three or four hundred prescriptions. I made some good friends there. A couple of the technicians had worked there for fifteen to twenty years, and most were friendly and fun. Other than the commute and long thirteen-hour days, it was a good job.

Not long after I had started at Economy Drug, I received the official sentence from Judge Hood. I would have to serve four weekends in jail during March and part of April. The judge said that he wasn't letting me by with just probation. He felt like I had a serious problem, and he wanted me to do some jail time to think about it. He lectured me quite extensively, and I said "yes, sir" to him at each break in his sermon. I was okay with the weekends in jail. Up to that point, there had been no guarantees as to what my sentence would be. Technically, I could have been given six months to a year in jail. There had been one scare for me earlier in the year as the specifics were getting worked out. It had come to the prosecutor's attention that due to my being a pharmacist and being in a "position of trust," my federal sentencing guidelines were different. It looked like I may have to serve some time after all! Since he had made me the promise of probation though, the prosecutor worked it out by dropping a count or two of my charges to get me back to where probation was an acceptable minimum sentence. Our first child was due in May, so I would get my sentence out of the way before delivery time.

I was assigned to a probation officer named Chad. Chad was actually a couple years younger than me. He was quiet, easygoing, and friendly. He never lectured me or talked down to me the way I would have expected a probation officer to do. He was always very respectful and straightforward. Everything was explained to me in detail—when I would report, how I would report, and what I could and could not do. It sounded, at first, like I would be on a short leash. It turned out to be fairly unobtrusive though. I only had to visit him for the first few months. Then all I had to do was fax him once a month and call every once in a while.

One summer while I was still on probation, I was vacationing in Myrtle Beach with my family. We went to Ripley's Aquarium one afternoon, and I had, of course, had several beers. Out of slightly less than 300 million people populating the United States, I ran into Chad at the aquarium, six hundred miles from either of our homes. I was very careful to keep my distance from him as we said hello. I am quite sure that he smelled the booze. I am quite sure that he could not have cared less.

I would report to Chad in person on a regular basis, and I would serve four weekends in jail. The judge would allow me to be on work release so that I could keep my job at Economy Drug. I worked it out with Ron, the other pharmacist, to work every weekend while I was doing my time so that I could get out on work release on Saturday and Sunday of my jailed weekends. He was all too happy to take all those weekends off. I was all too happy to work them. I can hear him now, explaining to his wife why he gets all the weekends off, "My new partner at the pharmacy needs to work all the weekends because he is serving time in jail for stealing narcotics and wants to be out on work release during the day."

I recall one of the technicians asking me shortly after I began working at Economy Drug how I was able to work around *all those drugs* after having such issues with them before. "I'm scared straight" was my answer. I would eventually learn that if a person is a true addict, this is not possible, at least not for any appreciable amount of time. Within ten weeks of starting my job there and before ever serving my first minute in jail, I was drinking and using again. I had decreased my visible drinking to oblige my wife and others, and I wasn't using to the same extent that I had been the year before. I had it under control now. It would be different this time. This time, the *snake wouldn't bite me.*

A short time before I was to begin my weekends in jail, I went to my doctor and explained to him that I was going to have to spend four weekends in jail, and I *needed* some Ambien to help me sleep. He was familiar with my situation, and he gave me a prescription without hesitation. With a doctor's prescription, I could use as much Ambien as I wanted, and I was covered if asked to pee in a cup. My manipulation skills were ever so sharp.

The first Friday that I had to show up to jail, I worked until 9:00 p.m. and then drove straight over to the jail parking lot. There I downed a couple beers quickly and popped a couple of Ambien tablets. I was processed, strip-searched (which included pulling my butt cheeks apart for a deputy), and then taken to a jail cell with twenty bunk beds in it and thirty to thirty-five guys. The lone commode was stainless steel and sat where everyone could see you do your business. I selected a top bunk bed since that was the only one available. I quickly made friends with some of the guys and was invited to play cards with them. We played spades, tonk, and some kind of dice game. It was apparently against the rules to have the dice in there, but somebody had managed to get their hands on them, and we just kept our eyes out for the guards and hid the dice when necessary. We played games until way up into the early hours. Unfortunately, my buzz wore off too quickly. I mentioned to the guys that I was a pharmacist and that I had popped a couple of pills before coming in. I had celebrity status instantly. They suggested that maybe I could sneak them in little dope to help them sleep too. I told them I would see what I could do upon my return to the jail after work the next day.

The next morning, I got up, showered, and banged on a two-way speaker to let them know that I needed to get out for work release. I would work 8:00 a.m. to 9:00 p.m., and then I had to show back up at the jail. During the day at work, I gathered up a few Xanax and some Ambien to take back to the jail with me. I had seen movies and heard stories of people smuggling drugs inside condoms by . . . well, you've seen the movies too. It wasn't easy or fun, but I did it. That's all I'll say about that. I also bought some chewing tobacco and a couple cartons of cigarettes. My new friends at the jail would appreciate the gifts.

I was a little nervous as they checked me in the jail, but it went smoothly. Once inside, I had to go sit on the stainless steel commode and extract the party gifts that I had smuggled in. That was unpleasant and no easy feat since it was in plain view of everybody.

The level of stupidity displayed by this act astounds and befuddles me today. I was spared going to prison by divine intervention only a few months before, yet at some point, I decided that it would be a good idea to sneak some drug contraband into a jail where I would only

have to stay a total of about eighty hours. Does this give *any* indication
of my level of insanity?

At the card table, I proudly announced that I had brought some
smokes, some chew, and some pills. "Don't ask," I told them before
the first one could ask me how I had managed to get the pills in. The
cigarettes and the chewing tobacco, I was allowed to bring in after
a quick check by the guard. Thereafter, I was welcomed each night
by getting high-fived and having a place made for me to sit at the card
table. It was actually kind of fun. Don't get me wrong, jail sucks. It
sucks bad! However, all I had to do was go in, play some cards while
doing some pills, smoke some cigarettes, and sleep until time to get
up and go back to work. Truth be told, I probably needed to do a little
more serious time in jail. That's not to say that I think it would have
fixed me or anything. I just didn't take my weekend status seriously.

On Sunday mornings, my boss, CC, would take me to breakfast at
Jerry's Restaurant. Then I would go to the pharmacy and work ten to
eight. After that, I would head back home to Hazard. I continued this
pattern each weekend until my time was done. Each time, I brought
just a few more goodies to jail with me.

On May 5, my son Cade entered the world. I was quite excited! Not
only was I excited that I had a son, but also that Darcey would be
spending the night at the hospital, and I would be able to drink
as much as I wanted at home that night! Yes! I snorted some pills
and drank blatantly while sitting right in my own recliner, baby! No
complaining, no bitching, no hiding, and no holding back. There
would be no evil looks or hug-sniffs. Nothing but unadulterated,
unhindered drinking for Daddy in his chair tonight! Where's my
remote control?

Darcey brought Cade home from the hospital. I had never even
held a newborn baby before. I hesitantly held Cade, and was afraid
of dropping him. Quickly though, I would learn how to cradle him
in one hand and a beer in the other.

I had essentially no responsibility toward my son whatsoever. I
worked, drank, slept, and emptied the cat's litter box. I worked

quite a few hours, drank as much as I could get by with, and slept half the day when I was off. I did such a terrible job of keeping the cat box emptied that the cat finally just started crapping in the floor because the box was so nasty. Lumps of poop on top of poop collected in the box because I was too high, drunk, or lazy to empty it. It was probably a combination thereof.

On several occasions, I would be sleeping late on my day off until eleven or twelve, and I would awaken to the sound of my brother-in-law mowing my grass. He couldn't stand to see it get so high, and I obviously wasn't going to do it. Ducking quickly back behind the curtain, I would roll over and sleep another hour or so.

Cade really didn't know me. I was so rarely around him. On the rare evenings I was off work, Darcey would ask me to watch him while she did the treadmill for an hour or so.

"I work all the time, and the last thing I want to do when I actually get some time off is babysit," I said smugly.

I am ashamed to admit that, but it's true. That was my view on it. How dare she ask me to do that! I am sure that I loved Cade even then, but when a person is in the grips of this disease like I was, they are not capable of real love. It's shallow at best. Being high is what you love. When you're not drunk or high, you feel too badly to love anybody. Any available energy is focused on getting high again.

Anyway, I just couldn't understand how she could ask me to do this after I had worked so hard all week. It's no wonder Cade didn't like me. When I was around him, he didn't pay me much attention. Darcey would hand him to me, and he would reach back for his mommy and cry. I just laughed it off, but honestly even then, it hurt. It never occurred to me that I might need to invest some time in order to be a daddy to him.

He wouldn't stay still when I was watching him. I would be trying to snort a pill in the downstairs bathroom, and he would take off up the steps toward Darcey as fast as he could go. Then Darcey would yell at me. It was very irritating and cumbersome to me.

Cade's first steps were toward a pretty green bottle that Daddy was holding. It was a Heineken beer. I thought it was so cool! Darcey did not find it amusing or cute. I couldn't wait for the day that we could drink one together.

Weeks and months went by, and I continued to drink and use more and more. I began to seek out drugs that I knew would not show up on a drug screen, putting my pharmacology training to good use. The fast-acting, short-duration sleeping pills became my preferred drugs. I started snorting them before bed to help me sleep. Then I ended up snorting them at work too.

Drinking was a complicated game for me. I had to juggle the amount I drank with what I thought I could get by with at home. If left solely up to Darcey, I would not drink at all. She knew that wasn't going to happen though, so there was an unspoken amount that was okay. I had a formula in my head that took certain things into account, such as her mood, how many drinks I had had in the past few days, whether or not I wanted sex when I got home, and the current position of the moon.

Darcey had been known to drink with me in high school and college and even some after we were married. She could hold her own at one time when it came to putting away some Wild Turkey. I loved when she drank. It gave me a free pass to get hammered. It also made her more amorous. Eventually, drinking became such an issue between us; she would drink when we would go out just to be able to tolerate me.

Driving home from work became a time for drinking and snorting pills. I was cautious in the beginning with fear of getting pulled over by police, but that didn't last long. At first, I would drive home from work in Pikeville, pull in the driveway, kill a beer, and then open one as I went into the house so I could explain my beer breath. Then I could get by with drinking two or three in front of her without too much consequence. It was just two or three beers, which wouldn't set her off too much, and I could always drink eight or ten more after she went to bed. Eventually, I graduated to slamming one before my neighborhood, one in the driveway, and then one on my way in the house. Next, I went to slamming one as I came across the Hazard bypass, one right before my neighborhood, one in the driveway, and then one on the porch. Then I would drink one at the county line, one on the bypass, one in the neighborhood, one in the driveway, and then the one on the porch. Finally, I graduated to just drinking the whole way home for seventy-five miles from Pikeville to Hazard. I kept a cooler in my car, and I popped a beer open as soon as I got off work and got to my car. In addition, I would snort Sonata along with the booze. For maximum using efficiency, I learned to multitask by learning to drive with my knees proficiently while snorting and crushing so that I didn't have to stop. I had gradually eased right back into the hell I had once barely escaped, throwing caution to the wind.

In spring of '98, my good friend George asked me to help him move from Chicago to LA. The plan was to load up a U-Haul trailer in Chicago and drag it behind George's Yukon for two thousand miles via the scenic route. We planned a scenic stop at the Grand Canyon, mountain biking in Moab, Utah, a visit with George's aunt in Denver, and a stop in Las Vegas for drinking and gambling with perhaps another biking trip.

I flew up to Chicago and got a ride to Skyview where George worked. We hit the bars that night and slept in the Yukon until morning. We went to his storage unit, loaded his stuff, and headed west. George took the first driving shift. I took some Ambien and went unconscious. About ten hours later, I came into consciousness as George punched me in the jaw hard. "I thought you were gonna help me drive, asshole!"

"Oh yeah . . . I can drive. Pull over," I answered drowsily and unenthusiastically.

"Shut up and go back to sleep, punk!" George was *not* happy that I had taken a handful of pills and crashed out on him, and he had no real intention of putting me at the wheel. He was just making a point. So I went back to Ambien land.

Eventually, I sobered up enough to drive a bit. In Moab, I was too sick to go biking. I had a sore throat, a fever, and felt like crap. I dropped him off with his bike and went back to the motel to drink beer and take a nap. George had an excellent ride. I drank and slept.

In Las Vegas, we went mountain biking just outside the city. It was gorgeous scenery with wild horses running free. I was so out of shape and hung over that it was an absolutely miserable ride. I had also worn cotton, which was not a good choice for the conditions. It seemed like we peddled uphill for thirty miles. I think it was actually seventeen. Finally, we reached the top. I was cold and exhausted. George informed me that the rest was downhill. *Thank God!*

I was so ready for some downhill. Finally, some payoff for the torturous, hard climbing! George took off ahead of me in a hurry. He was a much more experienced rider. I took off down the hill. Less than a quarter mile into the downhill single track, I hit a rock, flipped over the handlebars, and landed facedown in the mud. When I picked my bike up, I had a flat tire. I had no patch kit or extra tube, so I began the long journey of walking my bike out of the mountains about five miles. Beer. I needed beer.

I don't remember much of the trip. It could have been an awesome vacation driving cross-country with my best friend, but my addiction was more important. I wasn't there to help him at all. I was there to get as wasted as I wanted without my wife or family there to give me crap. I was more of a hindrance to him than a help since I was drunk, high, or passed out almost the entire time. We went to some incredible places, and I have no memory of them. I do remember seeing one picture of me standing with my pants at my ankles taking a piss on a statue of Ronald Reagan in the middle of some park in Illinois. Nothing against President Reagan, I just had to go apparently.

In the early part of 2000, I was released from probation a year early for *good behavior*. I had put on a deceiving veneer to the outside world, suggesting that I was doing great, was obeying laws, and was a model citizen. On the inside, I was lying, cheating, stealing, using, and hurting. I had faces that I put on for every occasion. There was the family face, which conveyed a hardworking man, providing for his family by working many hours each week. There was the church face, which suggested that I was a dedicated Christian man that sang in the choir, sang solos with my sister, and was in church every Sunday. The coworker face gave the impression that I was an easygoing pharmacist that simply liked to party a little and had a great sense of humor. Then there was the guy-on-probation face that communicated a repentant pharmacist that had made some little mistakes, but was walking the straight and narrow these days.

The early dismissal would turn out to be a lifesaver legally. Had I still been on probation when my final arrest occurred, I would have most likely sat in jail a while. Around this time, I applied to the governor of Kentucky to get my civil rights restored. In just a few weeks, I received a letter affirming that my right to vote and run for public office had been given back to me. I had never really cared much for politics or voting up to that point. When Election Day came, I would always ask my dad who to vote for and then I would go to the polls ready to punch whatever he suggested. When something is taken away from you though, it makes you want it that much more. Now I go to great lengths to make sure that I go vote.

Too much stress was my problem, I thought. So I employed some stress-relieving activities. I decided that fishing would be the answer. This would be one of many foolish attempts to solve the *stress* that troubled my daily life. I bought a new fishing rod and reel. I couldn't buy just any old rod and reel though. I had to have the $300 one so I could brag about how much I had paid for it while fishing with friends. The one with the very fancy reel would be what I needed. It was the most expensive one in the store that an old schoolmate named Terry owned in Hazard. He tried to talk me out of it since I had never used this particular type of reel, a baitcaster. I assured him that I possessed the expertise to learn quickly how to cast it. When I told him that all I had ever used before was a Zebco 33, he looked at me and smiled and said, "This ain't no Zebco 33."

The next Monday afternoon on my way to Lexington, I stopped beside the road to fish in a small lake that I passed each week. Yes, fishing would cure me. I had the answer now. If you're an alcoholic, you can relate to these types of endeavors that we thought would solve our "stress" problem. We try things like getting more exercise, only drinking certain types of alcohol, drinking only certain times of the day, getting more sex, etc. I parked my car, crossed the guardrail, walked through some pine trees, and put my tackle box down beside the water. It was a gorgeous, sunny, and warm day with blue skies and no wind. It was perfect fishing weather, and I had high hopes that this would be my new balance in my life. The water was clear and motionless. Tall cattails lined the water's edge, and a shale cliff rose to about forty feet on the side opposite the road. I put my favorite topwater bait on the line, a blue Rapala, and cast the line into the water. At once, an incredible mess of fishing line developed on top of my reel that resembled a giant afro. This is called a bird nest, I later learned. Apparently, you are supposed to put a little back pressure on the line as it releases, or this will happen. Apparently, it takes some skills to use one of these fancy reels effectively. If you've ever experienced one of these snarls of fishing line, you know what a disaster it can be. In seconds, I was yelling and cussing at the top of my lungs and stomping back to my car as angry and stressed as ever. I even thought of throwing the whole fishing rig into the lake. I still can't cast that stupid thing to this day so I gave it to my friend Aaron who makes it look easy.

I frequently wondered why I always seemed to fluctuate between depression and anxiety. I tried different things to lift my mood and calm the anxious feelings. It never occurred to me that my lifestyle of drinking heavily and snorting pills all day long had something to do with my mood swings. Add to that the confusion of living separate lives and having to keep all the lies straight in my head, and you can see my turbulent existence. I decided that I would try some Saint John's Wort, a herbal remedy for depression and anxiety. It didn't work, which I am sure will come as no surprise.

Another stress-management tactic I employed was exercising. I worked out at a place called Mike's Gym, just up the road from my house. I knew Mike well and also knew that he kept a key under the mat for access to the gym after hours. I began going late at night. Ah yes, more exercise would fix me! I'd stop and buy some beer before going because I'd need something to drink after working out, of course. The first few times I did this, I would do my workout and then go drink my beer on the way home. Then I got to where I would do most of my workout, and then enjoy a beer while doing my last sets. In a short time, I was taking a six-pack in the gym with me and drinking while working out. Finally, I was going in the gym with beer and just sitting at Mike's desk getting drunk and watching TV. Did I mention that Mike was a state cop? Stress-management failure number 20-something.

Other attempts to remedy my discomfort, restlessness, apprehension, stress, anxiety, depression, and agitation failed miserably as well. How was I to know that drinking and snorting pills daily had anything to do with the disquiet in my life? I switched drinks, changed drugs, exercised more, exercised less, bought gadgets, got massages, wrote poems, got new clothes, read books, studied pharmacology, got a motorcycle, had more sex, sang songs, and tried herbals. Nothing seemed to work. It was like switching seats on the *Titanic*; I was *still* going down.

My Monday-night counseling at the Morton Center was a group of doctors, nurses, and pharmacists that sat around and discussed various issues. It was an interesting group of people, all of whom had been required by their respective boards to attend. My initial visit was a survey of sorts to help them decide if I had a problem. This questionnaire asked several questions about drinking like, *Have you ever consumed more alcoholic beverages than you intended? Have you ever blacked out and not remembered things after drinking? Have you ever regretted things you did while you were drinking?* My answer was, "Yes, I went to college." I thought *everybody* experienced these things! Apparently not.

Eventually, I learned to say what they wanted me to say and act like they wanted me to act. I had no desire to be in recovery. I had no desire to be in counseling. After the session was over, I usually snorted a pill and opened a beer before getting out of the parking lot. One night, I excused myself halfway through the session, went to the bathroom, and snorted a Sonata. I was so proud of myself for pulling it off. I adored the endorphin rush that came with being devious and surreptitiously putting one over on the counselors. I smugly sat through the rest of the session, smiling to myself.

This was my life—paying for counselors that I consistently lied to, working long hours at a job where I was frequently high, living one high to the next while smiling to the outside world. Day in, day out, I ran on the hamster wheel.

I resented having to go to the counseling group. I had to pay for it—and urine screens too. It ran about three or four hundred bucks a month in addition to travel expenses to Lexington once a week. I was so clueless when it came to any kind of recovery. Once we had a new counselor named Terri. She had been there for a few weeks and had been kind of quiet up until now. I was getting ready to graduate and leave the group by virtue of having been going there for two years. We were just talking about what I had learned and what I was going to do when this new chick asked me a question.

"So how did you work step 3?" she asked. She simply wanted me to go over what I had done for me to consider this step "worked." We were required to have worked the first five of the twelve steps in order to graduate from the group. I had told them I was on step 6. It was a very reasonable question for anyone who had actually worked the step. It was a vicious attack in my eyes.

"What do you mean? I just *worked it*," I replied defensively. What I was thinking in my head was what the heck *was* step 3, and why was this newbie giving me a hard time when I was on my way out the door? I had read through the steps. I had heard them at the very few meetings I had gone to. They were always up on the walls at the meetings I went to. But I didn't have a clue what this woman was talking about. I attempted to cover my discomfort and panic with condescension and appalled anger.

"What did you *do* to work it?" she asked.

"I'm not sure I understand the stupid question?" I replied, getting visibly perturbed and irritated.

"I don't know how else to put it to make you understand the question," she said with a smile and a chuckle that also said she was on to my bullshit. This made me angry. It didn't take much for me to get angry though.

"That's just rude, and I don't have anything to say to you if that's the way you're gonna be. I don't need to sit here and get berated by you. You don't even know me!" I got up out of my seat and walked angrily out of the group. I was cornered. I didn't even know what step 3 was! I cleverly got out my PDA organizer. I had the steps in a file there. I pulled them up and read step 3 while walking down the hall: *Made a decision to turn our will and our lives over to the care of God, as we understood Him.* I formulated some BS about how I had "worked" the step and returned to the group. I lied about how I had prayed and had done some writing to work the step. I had heard of people doing such things when doing this thing called step work. I just hadn't understood her question, that's all. And then she had gotten so rude that I just needed to walk it off. Everything was cool. No harm done, just let me ease on out that door.

The board of pharmacy had apparently been backed up with cases in 1998 around the time I had gone through my ordeal in Hazard. It was several months before I received official word from them about what they were going to do as a result of my conviction. I thought it had blown over and they had forgotten me. The resolution came in the form of an agreed order, which is a contract of terms offered as a condition of allowing me to practice pharmacy. The offer was to suspend my license for six months! I was shocked! I had been practicing at this new job for months and now they wanted to suspend me?

I took the paperwork to my boss. He and his wife decided that I needed an attorney, and they would pay for it.

The attorney they hired for me was this guy who wore suits worth more than my car. No, really, I was driving a $500 Ford Tempo with body damage at the time. He smoked those really fat expensive cigars. His hair was slicked back with an entire tube of some kind of super-lawyer gel, and he walked with a confident swagger. We got together, discussed our game plan, and went down to Frankfort to deliver our demands to the board. We sat down in the office of Mr. Michael Moné, the executive director. I had prejudged him as a pompous and arrogant dictator. He was, however, the enemy.

By the time we left his office, he had knocked off a hefty fine and given me probation with the board instead of the suspension. The smug lawyer was so proud of himself. He took credit for the negotiations and the more lenient penalty. The truth is, Mr. Moné, would have done that for me if I had shown up by myself. It was simply standard practice for them to give that particular agreed order to a pharmacist in my position as an initial attempt to resolve the case. He wasn't trying to screw me. I didn't know that then. They were still working out the kinks in their standard procedures for licensees who had broken laws and such.

When I called to deliver the news to my boss, the cocky attorney had beaten me to it. He had brought Michael Moné, to his knees and forced him to be more lenient on me. The Cinnamonds were grateful.

The agreed order required me to take random urine screens, not be in charge of ordering narcotics, have regular random inventories of controlled substances, and several other requirements. It looked like a lot on paper, but it wasn't that much considering the circumstances.

It was good news. I had been worried about being out of work another six months. We were already in some pretty serious debt. The counseling and drug screens were getting expensive. I was paying the ARH $300 a month for my broken contract with them. I was driving 150 miles a day round trip to Pikeville. All my credit cards were behind. We were struggling financially, to say the least.

Pikeville was a hotbed for drugs as was Hazard. A week didn't go by that we didn't get a forgery at the pharmacy. Forgeries for Lortab, Soma, and Xanax were most popular. Entrepreneurial forgers would phone in their own prescriptions, and some of them were very convincing. I was a sleuth when it came to forgeries, and ruthless about busting them. It is ironic and slightly absurd that I was stealing drugs behind the counter, yet if you dare try to bring in a forgery, I'd go to great lengths to get you arrested.

Cert Cool Mint Drops, I had discovered, were about the same size and proportion as Lortab tablets. When I knew that I had a Lortab forgery, which comprised 95 percent of them, I would run the information through the computer to produce a label then place the Cert Drops in the bottle, charge the crook $55 cash, and send them away with a smile. Simultaneously, one of the techs would be on the phone with the local police. The offender would usually get picked up in the parking lot, and my techs and I had lunch paid for most of the remainder of the week compliments of Mr. Prescription Forger.

Occasionally, the forger would be quite angry after being released from jail. On several occasions, I received telephone threats of bodily harm. I didn't tolerate these verbal threats very well. I was a walking volcano just looking for a reason to explode. I was angry about everything and nothing. Guilt disguised as anger often fueled my tirade and justified the explosive retorts to these victims of my charade behind the counter. After being told that they were coming down to kick my ass, my blood would boil, and my heart would pound. I would take the phone receiver to the back of the shelves away from the ears of customers, and tell the threatening ones in colorful words that I got off work at 9:00 p.m., and I would be more than happy to meet them in the parking lot. I meant it. I was just looking for an outlet to direct my justifiable anger. I thought I was indestructible, and I wanted to fight. I wanted trouble, and these rednecks were disrespecting me. Furious exchanges took place while I hovered behind the shelves, screaming my own threats into the receiver.

Since I was a convicted felon, I was not allowed to be in possession of a gun. I am thankful that I didn't carry one during this segment of my life. On nights when I received these threats, I would buy a roll of quarters to carry with me out to my car in case I needed to hit somebody. My adrenaline would be pumping when I hit the door to leave work. I'd scan the parking lot for strange vehicles. I was ready to crush somebody. I was ready to unleash a fury of displaced anger on these verbal threat-makers. My guilt for being a thief, liar, addict, and a failure fortified, justified, and rationalized my desire to pummel another human. These guys were just like me though. I was doing the exact same thing, only I had a key to the pharmacy, and they didn't. The same failures and defects that I carried with me were the same failures and defects my would-be adversaries shouldered. We were both angry self-medicating addicts. None of the threat makers ever actually showed up to make good on their promises. I was always a little disappointed. This is yet another situation where God was watching out for me.

One guy actually came back in the store after I dispensed the Certs to him. He proclaimed that the Lortabs we dispensed were wrong, that we had dispensed the wrong thing to him. Again, with very colorful language, I called him the equivalent of a dim-witted fool and advised him that his prescription was a forgery, and some of Pikeville's finest were on their way to discuss it with him. He quickly turned and bolted for the front door.

In August 1999, a local car dealership in Pikeville, Deskins Motors, was going to give away a brand-new black four-wheel drive Dodge Durango. During the spring, they were promoting the giveaway all over the radio and driving the Durango around town. They had placed boxes all around the local three counties of Pike, Floyd, and Perry to put chances in. I decided that I was going to win this Durango. For three months, I devoted nearly every free minute of my time to filling out chances. I would stop by the various businesses where the boxes were, grab a pad or two (or eight if nobody was looking), and fill them out at work and at home. Some of them I highlighted, some of them I colored, and some of them I wrote things on the back like "pick me." Then I would fold them and place them in the boxes. I did this religiously and obsessively for the months leading up to the drawing. I even handed out chances to family members and had them fill out books at a time.

On the day of the drawing, Darcey and I drove over to Pikeville. It was a Saturday, and I was off work but scheduled to work Sunday. The drawing would take place at midnight. At about 11:30 p.m., they began to draw ten names from the back of a pickup truck as a crowd of people stood around. My name was one of the ten. That was no surprise since I could see several of the chances with my name on them floating around the bed of the pickup as I stood there.

The ten people whose names had been drawn were taken inside the dealership where ten numbered manila envelopes awaited us. I selected number seven. We got in line according to the number on our envelope. We opened them, and each had a key. I quickly noticed something about my key. It was scratched and weathered. I casually walked up and down the line, checking out everybody's keys. They all had that freshly cut shimmer to them, and no weathered scratches from being put in and out of an ignition. I had the key that went to that Durango. I was sure of it.

At midnight, we began to take our turn at attempting to start the engine on the Durango with our keys. A radio station was covering the event live, and we had to wait for the guy with the microphone to tell us when to turn the key and try it. By my turn, six people had tried their key and had no luck turning over the engine. That meant there were only three more people other than myself that even got to try, but they had dummy keys. I had the real one, and I had a death grip on it.

When it was my turn, I sat in the driver's seat. The MC guy was blabbering something into his microphone. While he wasn't looking, I slightly turned the key over, just far enough to see if those lights on the dash would light up. They did! I had just quietly confirmed that I was going to win a thirty-two-thousand-dollar vehicle this night!

When the guy gave me the signal, I started the engine and pumped my fist in the air with a loud yell when the engine roared to life. I was indeed the winner!

There was paperwork that I had to fill out before I could leave with the Durango. With beer sales stopping at 1:00 a.m., I was getting concerned that I wouldn't be able to buy beer if I didn't hurry and get out of there. Darcey left with Cade, who was just over a year old at the time, and drove to the motel. I quickly finished the paperwork and got to a store just in time to by beer. I bought a twelve-pack to celebrate.

At the motel, Darcey and I got into a huge fight over the beer I had bought. She just didn't understand that it was necessary to drink in celebration of such an occasion. She never really understood these things very well. Another moment destroyed that should have been celebratory.

The next day, I proudly drove my new Durango to work. I parked it right in front of the door so the naysayers that I worked with would see I had won the drawing, in spite of their pessimism and doubt. It wasn't all of them, just a select few. It was particularly fun to rub it in with one of my technicians, who told me over and over how stupid I was for filling the chances out, that it was a waste of time, and that they had already decided secretly who was going to win that truck. She could be pessimistic like that sometimes. I parked just as close to the door as I could so that she would be sure not to miss it when she came in. When I said something about it, she wouldn't even look at me while forcing out an insincere *congratulations.*

Pharmacy inspections were a part of my agreed order. At least twice yearly, an inspector would show up to check out the pharmacy and count some controlled substances. The board inspector that came to do my inspections and inventories was a bit younger than me. She was always quite nice and respectful. It made me nervous at first when she would come just because of whom she represented. Later, it made me nervous for different reasons. One reason was that I was using. She would walk into the pharmacy, and I would start to sweat, and my heart rate would rise. I knew that she didn't usually count the particular drugs that I was using, but I never knew for sure. Occasionally, I would be high when she would show up. I tried to keep from making eye contact on those days. There was always the possibility that she could ask me to pee in a cup too. She had the authority to do that.

The other reason I eventually got nervous was that somebody was stealing OxyContin from the pharmacy right under my nose. There were a couple of occasions where some Lortab was taken too. I had a guy working in the pharmacy that was a pre-pharmacy major. He was very friendly and eager to learn. He would come in to work and immediately get me a cup of coffee, a snack, or whatever else I wanted with a smile and enthusiasm. Every Thursday morning, after he had worked Wednesday night, I would be missing an entire bottle of OxyContin of one strength or another. That is a lot of schedule 2 narcotic to be missing! It took us a while to figure out who was doing it, but eventually, we pieced it together. It scared me to death because I was sure that the inspector, and perhaps my employers, would think it was me. I was using at the time, and I took pills here and there, but not an entire bottle of a schedule 2 narcotic! How dare he steal drugs from the pharmacy (insert sarcasm voice for previous sentence)!

The owners didn't quite know how to handle it. Eventually, they brought in a professional polygrapher and demanded everyone take a polygraph. He failed miserably although they never did get him to confess. They got him to admit to stealing some baseball cards and fired him based on that. Charges for stealing narcotics were never filed. Since they had tested him first and found their thief, I didn't have to take it. *Sigh!*

December 31, 1999, I had tickets to a Mellencamp concert in Indianapolis at Conseco Fieldhouse. I am a huge Mellencamp fan, and I had purchased tickets through the fan club. My son Cade had gotten a fever at the last minute, and Darcey decided to stay home. Darcey's mom, stepdad, and another couple had gotten tickets too, and so we all drove up to Indy for the show.

On the way up, we stopped at a place to use the restroom. In the men's room, I peeled off the back of a 50 mcg Duragesic patch and slapped it on my stomach. It delivers 50 mcg of fentanyl per hour directly through the skin. Duragesic patches are for people that have a very high tolerance for narcotics. It is normally used for cancer patients who are terminally ill, or for patients with terrible chronic pain. For people who are not tolerant, it can be deadly since narcotics slow the respiratory rate. Can you see what might happen to a person wearing one of these who drinks a few beers and then passes out? They go to sleep and never wake up.

Later at the Spaghetti Factory in Indianapolis, we were eating dinner and waiting for five o'clock to roll around. That was when we could pick up our tickets across the street at the Conseco Fieldhouse will call. I was wearing my sweatshirt that Darcey had gotten me for Christmas. It was black with white writing that said Pick Me 2 Sing. The white writing was lined with white Christmas lights that connected to a battery pack I kept in my pocket. With the flick of a switch, I was a walking billboard. As I walked to our table, a lady stopped me and read my shirt. She was in her fifties and was wearing John Mellencamp backstage passes around her neck. She smiled as she read my shirt. "I'm John's house manager, and I love your shirt! I will see him before he goes onstage, and I want to tell him to look for you. Where are you sitting?"

"I don't know yet. I have to get my tickets at five to find out," I replied.

"Well, let me know when you get them," she said.

I was elated! I had gotten a step closer to actually getting to live one of my dreams of getting to sing on stage with Mellencamp. I decided at that moment that I would drink the one beer that I had ordered, but none after that. I wanted to make sure I remembered this night.

At five minutes before five, I went across the street to get our tickets. I stood in a short line that led up to one of those folding tables where the fan club staff was sitting and handing out the tickets. I approached the table with my ID in hand and told her my name. She handed me an envelope with my name on it, and I turned and started walking away. I opened the envelope while I walked to look at the tickets. The tickets said they were row A. My eyes opened wide, and I turned and ran back to the table. I showed the girl my ticket and said, "This says row A. Does that mean what I think it does?" I said a little frantic. I knew that sometimes there's like a row AA, BB, CC that is the real front row.

"You got 'em, sweetie. They're front row," the girl behind the table replied.

I let out a loud woohoo! I ran across the street to show the gang our seats. Also, I made a stop at the house manager's table to show her my seats. She assured me that John Mellencamp would know about me and my sweatshirt.

Still wearing the Duragesic patch, I was feeling empowered and energetic. My eyelids were drooping a little bit, and I felt like every hair on my body was standing on end. The steady stream of narcotic fueled me.

Excited to visit our VIP seats, we got to the show early. Security guys hesitantly let me in the building with my ensemble of wires and batteries attached to my person. If I were to try to get into a show today wearing a gadget like that, they would send me away, arrest me, or a bomb squad would tackle me. September 11, 2001, changed all that. Along the way to our seats, several guys checked our tickets. Finally, we arrived. Just as promised, we were four feet from the stage on the front row.

John came out to a song called "Dance Naked." All the lights were out as John and his band filed out from the rear of the stage. In the dark of the arena, there were only two things that could be seen—cigarettes of the legal and illegal variety glowing randomly about the crowd, and then there was me on the front row, lit up like a small Christmas tree. Mellencamp didn't have a chance to miss me. He came out and looked right at me. Then he pointed and smiled as if to say, "Cool dude, I like it." Or maybe he was saying, "Dude, get a life."

I knew at this moment that the chances of my getting to get up there on the stage were very high. Would he recognize me on the front row and then pick somebody else? No way! I was in! I actually began to get nervous. I didn't sing to all the songs as he played them because I didn't want to lose my voice. It was a waiting game now. I was part of the show.

I was feeling no pain. The patch continued to release fentanyl, and I had reached a steady state of narcotic in my bloodstream way higher than any non-cancer person should ever have.

The song of promise finally rolled around. When the band began the first few chords of "Hurt So Good," my anxiety went up another notch. I was maybe two minutes away from the moment I had been waiting for! I didn't take my eyes off him. At the spot in the song where there is an instrumental solo and where I had seen John select the lucky fan in the past, it happened. He came over and pointed to me. I was ready. I had been ready for hours! I had been ready for years! I approached the chest-high stage and jumped up to put my forearms on the edge. Unfortunately, the security guard had not seen John point at me. He grabbed me and removed me from the stage. John came over and told the guy it was okay to let me up while the band continued to play a loop, awaiting my presence. John gave me a hand onto the stage. Standing on the stage, I looked over at Brother Mellencamp. He handed me the wireless microphone and did a thing with his hands opening toward a spot in the middle of the stage as if to say, "You're on! It's all yours!"

I went into autopilot at that point. I had done this a million times in my head and in my dreams. I'm not exaggerating. I had planned this moment for a long, long time, secretly practicing in bathrooms, elevators, and other private areas.

I took my spot, and the band revved up the crescendo leading into my newly assigned solo. I began singing to the eighteen thousand fans, and my personal dancer John Mellencamp. "Hurt so good. Come on, baby, make it hurt so good! Sometimes love don't feel like it should. You make it . . . hurt so good! Hurt so good. Come on, baby, make it hurt so good! Sometimes love don't feel like it should. You make it . . . hurt so good!" During my singing, I thought of my friend George when he had his Mellencamp experience two years prior, and how he had danced while he was singing. I wasn't going to be outdone, so I danced. I looked over at John, and he was smiling and dancing.

I thought about Darcey. I really wanted her to get to see this. She knew what this meant to me, and she would have loved to have been there. Although with her being absent, I was free to drink and behave how I wanted.

As I handed the microphone back to him, I gave him a hug and told him thanks. My eighteen thousand fans cheered for me as I exited the stage, or at least that's the way *I* remember it. My mother-in-law and her husband, Randy, were having a pep rally for me in the front row. Janie said something to me, but it was way too loud to understand, and my eardrums were shot. Onstage, the music had been surprisingly loud.

At the last note of the song, John came over to where I had returned to my seat and gave me five and a wink. Dream lived.

Now . . . time to drink! Enough with this sober crap. After the show, as we were leaving the arena, I was stopped no less than twenty times by people wanting their pictures made with me, wanting to congratulate me, asking for my autograph, and telling me what a great job I did up there! One guy told me he thought John was still singing when it was actually me. I'm not making that up. Maybe he was really drunk, but that's what he said! It's funny because after about twenty minutes of that, I was already feeling the pain that real celebrities feel. I was ready for those people to leave me alone. In less than half an hour, I had already gotten sick of being a "celebrity."

That night we partied hard. I mean, hey, I had just sung with John Mellencamp! I ran into several people throughout the evening that had seen me on the stage and wanted to buy me a shot or a beer. If I had known how dangerous it was for me to be drinking so heavily with a constant infusion of fentanyl from the patch oozing into my body, I probably . . . well, I could have . . . . ah heck, I would have done it anyway. I never was one to heed such warnings. I will say that I have read about many deaths due to fentanyl patches in the past few years. People would apply the patch, go to sleep, and stop breathing. Now there are some very specific warnings on the packaging about the dangers. I can't say that it would have mattered had I known these things though. Obviously, I wasn't a very cautious person.

I didn't die that night. We drove home to Hazard on Sunday. On Monday, I got a call to go drop a random urine screen. I went into a panic. I had used all weekend, and my blood was saturated with fentanyl. I called my friend Ed and begged him to help me. He met me in the parking lot of the place I had to go for the screen. He peed into a sandwich baggie for me, and I tucked that into my pants to take into the lab. In the lab's bathroom, I simply poured Ed's pee into the sample cup. He had assured me that his was clean, and I had no reason to think otherwise. It worked. I had a clean test. Life is so complicated being a drug addict.

As mentioned above, at one of the shows that I went to in 1997 in Chicago, my good friend George Fitz got to get up on stage with John and sang. It was sort of a tradition with Mellencamp that for the last verse of "Hurt So Good," he would pull a fan up on stage and let them finish the song. In Chicago, on April twenty-second, it was George's turn.

We were in the second row. Underneath his shirt, George was wearing a Camelbak hydration pack filled with margarita. It's like a small chest pack with a bladder insert, normally used by cyclists to carry water on long rides. We all took turns sucking George. There was no alcohol for sale at this venue. George walked in the place unchecked. He just looked a little more buff tonight.

I was my usual unruly self. At one point, I nearly got kicked out for having sneaked a camera in. When the security guy took it from me, I let him know what I thought about him and his rule. George had to beg him to let me stay. Finally, I agreed to settle down.

When "Hurt So Good" was playing, John came over and pointed in our direction; it wasn't quite clear which one he was pointing to, but the next thing I knew, George's foot was on my shoulder. He used me to climb over the front row and get on stage with Mellencamp.

George is extremely smart, handsome, and fun; but he's about as coordinated as a duck-billed platypus. His singing and dancing abilities are quite lacking, to say the least. He couldn't carry a tune in a box. His dancing is even worse. This night though, he gave it everything George Fitz had. He ran back and forth across the stage, kicking his legs high into the air and belting out the lyrics in a colorful, charismatic fashion. He didn't hit one single note right, but it was one of the most beautiful things I have ever seen and heard. I was screaming to the top of my voice to anybody that would listen beside me, behind me, and in front of me, "That's my best friend, George, up there! He's awesome!"

I was joined on this trip by two coworkers, Dave and Christy. If ever given the opportunity, I am betting that they wouldn't care to join me again. They ended up babysitting me on more than one occasion during our four days there. The last night we were there, I got so ridiculously drunk on tequila that I didn't even remember going back to George's apartment. George lived on the third floor of an old apartment building. I was carried up the steps because I couldn't walk. Apparently, while being carried, my wedding band slipped off my finger. It wasn't noticed at the time.

The next morning, I was suffering from one of the worst hangovers I ever had. I couldn't lift my head or open my eyes. Christy and Dave had to pack my things for me. When I realized my wedding band was gone, I told them I wasn't leaving until we found it. After searching the entire apartment—not me, of course, because I couldn't move—Christy remembered hearing something as we were coming up the steps. She disappeared and returned with my ring. I was so relieved.

Darcey had been unable to join us since she was in Saint Louis at Lutheran Medical Center. She was staying in their eating-disorders program for two weeks. I didn't see any reason why I should waste my Mellencamp tickets and cancel my trip just because she was in a lockdown facility being treated for life-threatening eating disorders. I saw it as a perfect opportunity to party as hard as I wanted without her interfering. Let me repeat what I just said, not for your benefit, but mine. I left my wife in a treatment center for eating disorders and flew to Chicago to go to three Mellencamp shows, three nights in a row. While she was locked away in a hospital, I partied just as hard as I could. Wow, what a dedicated and loving husband.

On the trip down to take her there in April 1997, I had a bag of cocaine. We drove to Louisville to catch a plane, and I snorted cocaine the whole way down. I had told Darcey that I had diarrhea so that I could stop and do another line every twenty to twenty-five minutes. When we got up to catch the plane the next morning in Louisville, I felt like hell. I was out of coke and out of gas.

During the check-in process in Saint Louis, all I could think about was getting back to the airport so that I could drink a large glass of the strongest bourbon they had. Never mind my wife was in such a delicate condition that her counselor felt inpatient treatment was essential. Never mind I was leaving her at this completely foreign and terrifying place with a bunch of strangers where she would stay at least two weeks.

At the airport, I began to drink away the pain brought on by the cocaine, depleting my stores of dopamine. My nerve terminal was depleted, and my brain's reward pathway was in desperate need of repair. Alcohol would have to babysit me for a while. On the plane, I drank everything they would give me as fast as they could bring them. I was achy all over and had no energy whatsoever.

The next few days, I would get to drink as I desired since Darcey would be locked away in Saint Louis. I was looking forward to it. This is not a normal kind of thinking. I realize that now.

When you're constantly snorting pills that zap your memory and you have days that you don't remember anything at all, you tend to lose your inhibitions and get loose with the tongue. I apparently let some concerns slip while talking to my sister one night in the middle of a drug-induced blackout. I don't know exactly what it was I said, but the insinuation was that maybe being forced to go to these Narcotics Anonymous meetings and counseling sessions wasn't such a bad idea since I was finding myself having some difficulties with these substances *occasionally*. Perhaps I had a problem after all. My sister translated that as a cry for help, and she was right on the money.

FAMILY INTERVENTION

We thought we could find an easier softer way, but we could not.

—*Alcoholics Anonymous*, Big Book,
Chapter 5, "How It Works"

Drug-induced blackouts had become common. I would work entire thirteen-hour shifts in the pharmacy and have no recollection whatsoever the next day.

One particular day, a little old lady came in and said to me, "Honey, you know yesterday when we were talking about my Cardizem prescription?"

"Yeeeeaah . . . sure," I answered. I had zero recall of that conversation. We had discussed whether or not she would be able to open this particular capsule and take it in applesauce since she had trouble swallowing large capsules. Nothing. I didn't remember seeing her the day before because I didn't remember being *at work* the day before. I worked as a pharmacist for thirteen hours, preparing patients' medications, counseling them on their prescriptions, taking phone prescriptions from doctors and nurses, and probably filled close to three hundred prescriptions; and I couldn't piece together any memory of the day. This happened on several occasions. Somehow I managed to never hurt or kill anyone while practicing in this state of mind. Lucky for me, God is also a competent pharmacist.

One day, as I worked, I found out to my dismay that I had ridden my motorcycle to work the previous day. I had no recollection of that happening. I had ridden my motorcycle to work on several occasions. I enjoyed riding. It was a rush. I enjoyed combining the adrenalin rush of fast motorcycle riding together with drugs. One of my more dangerous activities was to mix riding my motorcycle at 120 mph with inhaling of nitrous oxide from a whipped cream can. I would get my speed up to the desired number and then insert the nozzle of the whipped cream can through the face opening of my helmet and take a big bong hit of nitrous oxide. Holding a steady course at over 100 mph, I leaned forward over the gas tank of my Suzuki 750 crotch rocket for optimal aerodynamics while enjoying an almost out-of-body experience.

On yet another occasion, I was putting on my coat to head home after work. The inside chest pocket of my coat had a piece of paper in it. I pulled out a speeding ticket that I had apparently received two nights prior in Martin County on Highway 80. I didn't remember any of it. I can't believe I didn't get taken to jail that night. The drive home to Hazard was a frequently misplaced memory. Once in the car and on my way, I got high the whole way home. I took pride in the fact that I could drive with my knees while holding a CD case in one hand and the snorting straw with the other hand while doing a line. If it was a pill that needed crushed first, I would remove the metal portion of my ashtray in my Nissan Altima and flip it over. On that hard surface, I would place the tablet to be crushed. Then I would lay a dollar bill over the tablet to keep broken pieces from going everywhere and then crush away with the back of a screwdriver or other handy instrument. Further reduction of the powder and polishing was accomplished with the trusty credit card. All this without sacrificing any travel time. Impressive, huh? Not quite résumé material.

Prior to the family intervention, I had conceded to myself and a select few others that I was having a problem quitting the drug Sonata. One day after work, I went home without the usual pocketful of the stuff. I was determined to quit. I had a few while at work and put three in my pocket in the event of an emergency while I was trying to quit. I snorted those before I ever even got home though. I told Darcey of my plan, and we went about our usual evening and went to bed. At about 3:00 a.m., I woke up in a cold sweat with feelings of panic and fear that were making my heart beat out of my chest. An incredible feeling of doom enveloped me, and I was gasping for breath. I sat up in bed and started downstairs for some unknown reason. My legs were weak. I just knew I was dying. I got to the bottom of the steps and couldn't remember why I had started down there in the first place.

Intense fear exploded within me. I started upstairs and couldn't walk. I crawled back up, step by step. When I got to my bedroom, Darcey sat up as she heard me saying, "Oh God, oh God!"

"Oh no, what's wrong, Jared?" she asked me.

"I don't know, I don't know! Oh God, I think I'm dying!" I replied. I had a hunch that it had something to do with withdrawal. I was in severe panic like nothing I had every experienced before.

"What do I do?" Darcey asked me in a panicky voice.

"I don't know, just hold me," I answered. Yes, I know that sounds like a cheesy soap opera. "Oh, just hold me, and I shall live!"—but that is exactly what I said, and it's exactly what I wanted. I was as terrified at that point in time as I have *ever been* before or since. If you were to tie me down to some railroad tracks where I could see a train coming toward me at full steam, the panic and fear from the approaching locomotive couldn't compare to what I felt that night. Words don't even come close. I remember thinking to myself that *this* is exactly why some people put a gun to their head and pull the trigger without hesitation. I completely understood at that moment. Never before, and never since, but that night, I understood. I should have known that this was a temporary feeling. It's difficult to explain, but in that moment I couldn't anticipate it diminishing. For lack of a better description, I felt I was stuck there in that horrible moment. I would have gladly preferred death to spending time in that state of panic.

"Should I take you to the emergency room?" Darcey asked.

I declined. No way was I going to the hospital that fired me over stealing drugs to be treated for drug withdrawal! Never mind the little detail that I could be dying or about to start having seizures! My pride was so strong that I would rather risk death.

I had to have *something!* I was going to die! I remembered having a couple bottles of Jägermeister stashed in my car. Doesn't everybody have some Jägermeister stashed in their car for a Jägermeister emergency? I would have much preferred a trusty Sonata with its reliable calming effects, but booze would do in a pinch. I crawled and walked out to my car to found the bottles. It was two of those airport-sized servings, and I downed one of them immediately. I went back inside and drained the other one, still very anxious to feel some relief as I sat on the couch. A few minutes later, I felt the alcohol do its thing. Oh what a wonderful feeling that was! My heart rate slowed. The panicky feeling abated. I managed to make it upstairs and get back in bed. Darcey rubbed my head, and I finally went back to sleep. I remember thinking as I was drifting off to sleep that I would never ever, ever do that stuff again. It had scared me so badly that I was done! Done, done, done! If only I could have known that it's not that simple. If only I could bring into my consciousness with sufficient force the memory of the suffering from that night alone, I could quit drinking and using by sheer willpower. Within a week though, I was using again.

Back to the intervention. My sister told my brother, and he planned a trip to Hazard to confront me. The wagons were circled. My brother rolled into town on a Friday night. My mom had become suspicious that something was wrong with me. She pulled my brother's wife aside and asked, "Do you think Jared is using drugs?"

"That's why we're here," Amy answered, and the intervention ensued.

It was summer of 2000 on a Saturday, I got up fairly early to go down to my mom and dad's house for coffee. It was something I enjoyed doing on my Saturdays off, especially when we had family visiting. I stumbled down the path to the back door, and my brother met me as I opened the door.

"Mom knows about your drug problem, and they are upstairs telling Dad about it as we speak." Dizziness engulfed me. Where's the panic button? Or the escape button, yeah that one, where is it? Somebody throw me a life preserver or a fire extinguisher or an escape hatch! I didn't know what to say. I didn't know what to do. I just followed my brother into the den without a word, head down and eyes wide. If I'd had a tail, it would have been tucked between my legs. I wish that I could put into writing exactly what went through my head here, but I can't. I went into a sort of trance. Heck, there really wasn't any denying it at this point. Even the family members in the deepest denial were starting to see something was wrong.

We made our way into the living room, and I was seated on the couch. Mom was crying and telling me that whatever she had to do to get me help, she would do it. She loved me and would do anything at all to get me the help I needed. Then Dad came down the steps from his bedroom. He looked very weak and serious, and he walked slowly. He came toward me, got down on one knee, grabbed my hands, and said that he didn't know anything about this kind of stuff with drugs and addictions; but he loved me, and he would do anything to help me. He didn't finish before beginning to cry. I began crying, and I am sure the whole room was doing the same. I had only seen my dad cry one or two other times in my entire life. One time was when I was in high school, and Dad was in the hospital after having a heart attack. The doctors had told him that he was going to need open-heart surgery. When it was just family in the room, he cried and admitted that he was scared.

This was a pretty intense moment. I was surrounded by my family, telling me they loved me and that I needed help. I conceded that I had a drug problem. I had been suspicious for a while that this was the case. I would begin going to some NA meetings and get my life together. The bootstraps had been pulled. Jared was going to get his head on straight and get back on track! I flung my cape over my shoulder, ready to attack this problem! I would and could do this! New vigor gave me new hope. Strapped and loaded with willpower, I was ready to show this addiction who was boss!

My brother Eric then began to insist that I needed to go to an inpatient drug rehabilitation facility, preferably a thirty-day program, if not more. It was proven, according to him, that people couldn't usually be successful at overcoming these things without professional help. I figured he'd had just a little too much psychology training in college. Plus, this was Jared Combs we were talking about here. I was different! There are actually some statistics out there that say the odds of an alcoholic or addict quitting drinking or using on their own without professional help is one in fifty thousand. I didn't know this at the time, of course. If I had, I am sure that I would have felt absolute confidence in being the *one*.

"Oh no! I can't do *that!*" I exclaimed.

I began to explain all the reasons why it wasn't possible for me to go away to treatment. I would lose my license to practice pharmacy when the board of pharmacy found out. I would lose my job. What would Economy Drug do without me? How could I afford to go? How could I afford to take off work? People would find out. People would know I was a drug addict! I would be labeled! It's so ironic that we won't hesitate to steal or lie, but when it comes time to take a positive step toward recovery, we're all worried what somebody might think.

Being the good manipulator that I was, I convinced the family that I could do this on my own. They insisted that I tell my boss, CC, about my struggles and my plan to attend meetings of NA. He would need to know since he might need to cut my hours on days that I need to get to a meeting or do some counseling. I agreed to talk to him.

I planned on squeezing in a meeting of NA here and there, and I would talk to the counselor about my little problem. And so it went, I embarked on my endeavor to find an easier, softer way.

The counselor, Mike Spare, had tried several times to reach out to me. He offered to meet with me in his office one night after work to talk about my "drinking." I worked until 9:00 p.m. in Pikeville and wouldn't be home until 10:30 p.m. at best. That's assuming that no patients roll in at 8:50 p.m. with a bag of thirty prescription bottles. He had agreed to wait on me. This is something I didn't understand. *Why would he wait on me until ten thirty and then hang out with me and talk until midnight? What's in it for him? Was he gay or something?* He wasn't asking me for any money. I didn't get it. It turns out he just cared. What a concept.

When I eventually met with him, my biggest question was, "What do you do when you don't drink?" I just couldn't imagine going to a concert, to a ball game, or to any kind of a social event without drinking. He explained to me that, believe it or not, it was possible. Life could be full and fulfilling without alcohol. I did *not* believe him. How could one *possibly* enjoy life without drinking!

I was scheduled to work the next day after my intervention, which was a Sunday. I went in early to talk to CC, my boss. We opened at 10:00 a.m., and he was always in there early on Sundays, doing computer backups about an hour before. I told him that I had something serious that I needed to talk to him about. When I tried to get words to come out, I started crying.

Mr. C said, "Oh no, you're not quitting on me, are you? Do you have another job? How much are they paying you?"

"No," I said, "it's much more serious than that. I have been using drugs, and I can't stop. It's gotten pretty bad, and my family sat me down for a serious talk yesterday. They said I need to get help."

CC pondered this for a moment and proceeded to give me a pick-yourself-up-by-your-bootstraps speech. He said something about walking too closely to the edge of the cliff and how I just needed to take a step back. You just need to . . . blah-blah-blah. Just muster up some willpower, and beat this thing. He would help me however he could. I respected CC a lot. At the time, his speech gave me some hope and direction. It made some sense then. He honestly wanted to help me.

CC was a crotchety old dude with a rough exterior, but a big heart. He was a diabetic and didn't take good care of himself. His feet had sores on them that required him to see doctors almost weekly for antibiotics and debridement of dying foot tissue. His balance was terrible due to the foot sores combined with some inner ear problems. Some days he would be standing there, lose his balance, and have to grab the counter to keep from falling.

He chewed Red Man chewing tobacco. He reminded me of Ebenezer Scrooge in Dickens's *A Christmas Carol*. He came off to most people who worked for him like a mean old man. His drive for success and financial gain veiled the smile and conviviality that lay beneath. At times, we would get a glimpse of this affable side, but only very rarely. If he liked you, he really liked you, and he would do just about anything for you. That didn't mean that he wouldn't still be a grumpy old bastard to you if he felt like it on occasion, but if you needed somebody in your corner, you couldn't ask for a more loyal and steadfast friend. Not only was he loyal, but he was also very wealthy and well-known in Pikeville. He was the grand poo-bah of the Rotary Club and knew the governor of the state personally. He could make things happen in his little town of Pikeville.

He gave me a job the day I walked into his office after I had been indicted on federal drug charges and just released pending sentencing. Ninety percent of the charges had been dropped against me, but I had pled guilty to several counts of *obtaining a controlled substance by deception or subterfuge* (whatever that means) as a part of a plea deal where I would end up with three years probation and four weekends in the Pikeville jail. I told him all of this up front and also told him there was no guarantee I wouldn't have to go to jail since it was all at the judge's discretion. I wouldn't know until perhaps February what the official penalty was. He made me an offer. I had been front page of the newspaper and on the six o'clock news for about four or five months. Not many people were probably gonna jump to hire me. He told me that as long as I was trying to do the right thing, he would give me a chance. He reminded me of my mamaw (my great-grandmother on Mom's side). She always had a big place in her heart for those that were in and out of trouble.

Here's an example of Mr. C's kindness and generosity: One day, I had visibly been having a stressful day working at Economy Drug. I had been there probably about a year at this point. Apparently, I had been stressed for some time. I'm guessing it had something to do with all the narcotics I was snorting and booze that I was drinking. I don't remember what clued him in, but he asked me what was bothering me lately. I began explaining to him that I owed a large sum of money to the hospital from which I had been fired. I was making payments to them to the tune of about $300 a month. Since I had been arrested and fired, that was apparently a breach of my contract and the balance was due. It was a tough payment to make, and I was behind on almost everything.

He said, "Is that all you're stressed about? Money? Hell, I got plenty of that." He then hinted that maybe there was something he could do. He asked me exactly how much the payment was.

A couple weeks later, I was called back to the office. The secretary sat me down and explained to me that CC had arranged a monthly bonus to be added to my check in the exact amount of my payment that I made each month to ARH. Just like that, he gave me almost a $4,000-a-year raise just to ease my mind of financial struggles I had dug myself into. I cried. He was paying me a good salary, paid for 100 percent of my health insurance, and now he was throwing in a monthly $300 bonus just to help me out.

CC had no understanding of my problem, and neither did I at the time. I devised a plan of willpower and threw in some NA meetings for good measure, a plan that was destined to fail. It's just part of the recovery journey, always trying to find an easier, softer way until we get smacked with reality.

For weeks following the intervention, I tried to stay clean. I attended some Narcotics Anonymous meetings to satisfy my wife and fulfill my promises to my family, but I had no real desire to be there. I didn't think it was something that could help me. I was different. Those people were beneath me. I did get to know some of the people there eventually and cried to them regularly when the pain was enough. About half the time though, I would skip the meeting and go drink beer.

I recall the following scenario happening on several occasions during this period of *white-knuckle recovery*: I was driving to work from Hazard to Pikeville, a seventy-five-minute drive, at six thirty in the morning, to be sure and get there to open at eight. The whole drive, I am assuring myself that *I am not going to use today!* I mean it. Today is going to be the day I start over, and I will not get high when I get to work. I feel like hell. I used yesterday, but *not today!* I am confident, determined, and steadfast. But there is a dark side to my mind that takes over when I get within five minutes of the pharmacy. A new thought is imposed upon me without my conscious permission. *Yes, you are going to use today. As soon as you open the pharmacy, you will find the Sonata, open two capsules, and snort them.* It was like this disease monster had a remote control that operated my brain. Just for kicks, it would let me have some confidence in myself for a little while and then assert its domination. The feeling of being controlled scares me, and makes me angry, but at the same time I am exhilarated. I have a free pass to use now. The decision has been made. The Sonata promises to bring me the ease and comfort to which I have become accustomed. The fears and guilt that I bear will be forgotten, two capsule powders at a time. Anxiety will be gone. For this one more day, I will surrender to it, white flag in the air, snorting straw to my nose. Tomorrow will be different. Today is lost.

If you've battled addiction, you know exactly what I am talking about. You know what it feels like to be taunted and controlled by your addiction. You understand how it feels to have your confidence and hope stomped to death by an overwhelming and uncontrollable desire to either use or die. You know of the fallacious belief that tomorrow will be different. You know the defeat of having failed yet again.

The leader of the NA meetings I visited always made a quick statement before opening the floor for sharing. If you had used within the past twenty-four hours, they respectfully requested that you just listen and not share. I frequently had to look at my watch to see if I qualified to share. The girl chairing one night saw me refer to my watch, and she invited me to share anyway. I began to cry and tell them how I had failed again. I really wanted to stop using drugs. I truly wanted to be clean. I just didn't quite understand what that meant or how to get there yet. It seemed so far away from the realm of possibility. I couldn't fathom quitting forever. They told me to just not use *today*, and tomorrow, we'd deal with tomorrow. My reservation of exempting alcohol was one large barrier that I didn't comprehend at the time, and this was politely explained to me on several occasions by this group of addicts. They always invited me back though. They saw hope in me that I didn't. They had gotten beyond that point behind which there seemed no hope.

One of the readings at the beginning of each meeting made a statement that I didn't like or agree with.

> Thinking of alcohol as different from other drugs has caused a great many addicts to relapse. Before we came to NA, many of us viewed alcohol separately, but we cannot afford to be confused about this. *Alcohol is a drug.* We are people with the disease of addiction who must abstain from all drugs in order to recover.

Hmmm . . . nope. Don't like that statement. What else ya got?

Occasionally, I would get handed one of the six laminated pages to read before the meeting. When I would get the one that had this statement in it, I would quickly find somebody to trade with. I didn't tell them why, I would tell them I wanted a shorter reading or something. The truth was, I was probably going to Eddie's liquor store after the meeting to drink beer with him. I did not agree with the statement. Drinking and using drugs were two different things in my book. Nobody was going to tell me I couldn't drink! Drinking wasn't illegal! Drinking wasn't my problem!

Eddie would order special beers for me, whatever I wanted. I would pay him in advance, and they would be sitting back in the walk-in refrigerator of Hazard Liquor for me whenever I came by. We would sit and talk about how silly it was that Darcey suggested that I was an alcoholic.

In September of 2000, Dad and I decided to take a fishing trip to my cousin Matt's place in Ohio county. I had continued struggling with quitting drugs, and we thought that a little getaway might be helpful. We hopped in the truck and headed west for the weekend. I took nothing with me in the way of drugs. We had beer, of course, but no drugs.

On the trip down there, I got a headache that gradually got worse the farther west we went. My nose soon began bleeding as well. At this point in my life, I never got headaches unless it was hangover related. I wasn't hungover. With all the pills I snorted over the course of four or five years, I never had a nosebleed ever. I snorted lots and lots of powder up my nose, from crushed up Lortab, Xanax, and Percocet, to emptied capsules of Tylox and Sonata. I even snorted a Thorazine once. Occasionally, I played with some cocaine. I don't recall ever having a nosebleed though that wasn't caused by somebody's fist.

When we got to Matt's, I took a nap with tissue stuffed up my nose and an ice pack to stop the bleeding. Eventually, the headache was gone, and the bleeding stopped. We had a pleasant weekend as far as I can recall, and returned home Sunday afternoon.

At home, I was talking with my mom on the back porch before walking up the path to my own house. She asked me, "Well, honey, how'd you do?"

I knew what she was referring to. We had discussed my attempt to stay clean over the weekend to get me off to a good start. "I didn't use any," I replied.

"I'm so glad, honey. I prayed you could do it. I prayed that God would give you *headaches, nosebleeds,* or whatever it took to keep you from taking those stupid drugs."

There is zero exaggeration here. Those were my mom's exact words. My eyes must have been as wide as saucers. I looked at her with my mouth hanging open with bewilderment. "Mom, please think before you pray for things! I had severe headaches and a nosebleed on the way down there, and I was miserable!"

She just smiled and hugged me. My mom is a prayer warrior. When she talks to God, expect something to happen. When I need some serious prayer for somebody, even if she doesn't know them, I ask her to pray.

SPIRITUAL EXPERIENCE NUMBER TWO

The Epiphany

Half measures availed us nothing. We stood at the turning point.
We asked his protection and care with complete abandon.

—*Alcoholics Anonymous*, Big Book,
Chapter 5, "How It Works"

Remember the first part of the book where I was in the jail cell and I said those words out loud about being a drug addict and alcoholic? Who but God himself could bring on such an inspired understanding of one's own situation in such dismal circumstances and instill such hope where there would seem to be none? Only days earlier, I was drunk, rowdy, beat-up, and in complete denial of any problems with alcohol. Here I was though, in jail but hopeful about my future, with a new acceptance in my heart. Prayer works. Hope is a powerful thing.

A couple weeks before my arrest, I was hurting pretty badly. I had a couple of really bad days of blackouts, marital instability, and mental and physical torment; I was getting concerned and scared. Repeated attempts to stop using were unsuccessful. Week after week, I failed to take control of my using. Week after week, the disease laughed at me and taunted me with its domination. When things calmed down in the pharmacy one particular evening and my tech was on her break, I walked between the shelves of drugs, and knelt down to pray. I don't remember the exact words, but I asked God to *please help me*. I said that I couldn't do this anymore and that I needed help. I told God that I was hurting and scared and I would do whatever he told me to.

Here's what I remember about my last debacle and the ensuing days. It was a Wednesday night of October 4, 2000, and I was working at Economy Drug in Pikeville. I had worked there since January of 1998. I was planning on spending the night at a motel there in town since I was working a thirteen-hour day and then scheduled back in the morning at eight for another long day. That's what I normally did when I worked long days back to back like that. The reasoning on the surface was so that I could get plenty of rest between these long shifts. I lived in Hazard, which was about seventy-five miles and a drive of about an hour and fifteen minutes. The *real* reason for staying there was so that I could get as drunk and high as I wanted without my wife knowing and without her bitching and complaining about it. This was gonna be one of those nights.

I thoroughly enjoyed having a motel room to myself with some beer, narcotics, and maybe some sleeping pills, oh, and of course, some speed for the morning. I was my favorite drinking and using buddy. Most of the time, I would just hole up in the room, and I would be just as content as could be. I liked to get real good and drunk all by myself more than sharing the moment with anybody else usually. Sometimes, I liked to get out and hit a bar or two. Occasionally, some of the folks from work would want to meet at some local bar, and I would go there with them.

Once, I booked a night at the Landmark Hotel in downtown Pikeville. It was sometime in '99, maybe late '98. As I was crossing the parking lot, I recognized a gentleman in the parking lot of the hotel. It was one of the officers that had investigated and arrested me in 1997 over the ARH ordeal, Detective Layne. I passed him up without speaking because he was talking to another guy. We both nodded to each other. I thought that he might be working undercover, and I didn't want to blow his cover. I waited on the landing of the outside staircase for him to finish his conversation, and he came my way. I asked him if he remembered me, and he said he did. He asked how I was doing, where I was working these days, how my kids were, and so on. I told him that I had my life back together, was working hard, and was doing phenomenally well. Then he referred back to my criminal case of several years ago.

"You know, sometimes in our jobs, we have to do things that we don't enjoy," he began, "and your case was one of the difficult ones. I didn't feel like you had done all that you were being accused of, but I had a job to do." He said that he was glad to see that I was back on my feet, working, and raising my family. He continued with some other quite pleasant and sincere remarks, and we chatted for about ten or fifteen minutes out on the steps just one landing below my room. It's always interesting to me how we perceive people in one particular light, but under different circumstances, we see that they are entirely different. He was very amiable and down-to-earth as we spoke. We said our goodbyes and went to our rooms. I watched as the detective went to the room immediately next to mine on the left. How ironic, I thought. Then I went into my room, snorted a Tylox, and dedicated it to the detective. I took some very bizarre enjoyment in consuming narcotics only feet away from this cop in the next room. It was a peculiar delight for me.

The night I was finally arrested, I started using before noon. Due to the possibility of getting drug tested at any time by the board of pharmacy, I had developed a strange fondness for a specific sleeping pill called Sonata. It is a close cousin to Ambien and is in a capsule. The reason for this fondness was that Sonata could not be detected on a drug screen. Most drug screens are pretty specific for things like marijuana, opiates, benzodiazepines, and other common drugs of abuse. This didn't fall into any of those broad categories, although it was similar to benzos. Even if there was a screen that *would* detect it, the half-life is only about an hour. After five to seven half-lives, most drugs will be undetectable. So if I had gotten a call to go "drop," I would have simply stalled as long as possible and would have been perfectly clean by the time I got to the lab. Long story short, it's undetectable.

I remember well the day that the King Pharmaceuticals rep came into Economy Drug. She wanted to tell me about a new drug called Sonata for insomnia. I listened to her dialogue about the drug intently. It sounded like a wonderful drug, and yes, I would order some from our wholesaler immediately to have on our shelf. In the interest of our patients, I would even try some although I withheld this piece of information from the rep. I had already had an affair with Ambien, which was in the same class of drugs. Sonata was a powder in a capsule for my snorting convenience. It turned out to be a wonderful drug to snort. It was a small volume of powder with a slight sweet taste in the back of the throat. There was no burning of the nasal passages after snorting. Absorption across mucous membranes proved to be quite complete. Lastly, as a schedule 4, it would be unlikely to raise flags.

By lunchtime on October 4, I was high, thanks to King Pharmaceuticals' newest prodigy. Sometime in the previous months, I had confided in a couple of my technicians in yet another blackout that I was having a problem with this particular drug. They responded by hiding the Sonata from me daily. Any day that I was scheduled to work, the techs would take the bottle of Sonata and put it in some random spot behind another drug somewhere on the shelves. If we had a prescription for it, I had to leave and go to the breakroom after entering the data for the prescription into the computer. I didn't get to see the final product at all. After I entered it, they filled it and checked each other, and I was out of the loop. They didn't even trust me to touch the bottle. It became somewhat of a game for me to come in ten or fifteen minutes early in the morning to play "find the Sonata." I would search until I found it. It was like hunting Easter eggs every day! On this day, I had a bright idea that would circumvent their little protective plot against me. I just happened to remember the name of a patient that had a prescription for thirty Sonata capsules. I remembered that her insurance did not cover it, and she said she did not want it. It was no fluke that I remembered this actually. I wrote down all this information for this specific purpose when I realized she wasn't going to get it filled. I had just waited a couple days just to make sure. I refilled the prescription from of her profile and ran it as cash. When the label printed, my technician Linda looked over at me and pointed for the breakroom. I obeyed the unspoken directive. However, later, I simply pulled the bag from the will-call bin since nobody would be coming to pick it up. I pocketed the bottle of thirty capsules and threw away the bag. A drug addict will always find a way to get drugs. Oddly, I still feel a ripple of pride when I think of little personal drug addict victories like these.

My tech, Linda, told me one day that on days she knew I was high driving home after work, the first thing she would do in the morning was read the newspaper to see if I had been killed or arrested. Some days, she would leave work at five and wonder if she would see me ever again. She said that there was this vacant look I would get in my eyes when I got to a certain point of intoxication. Some days, she would notice me approaching this level, and she would tell me to go lie down somewhere. I would go back to the breakroom and lay my head down until she came and got me. The girls would fill the prescriptions without any pharmacist check whatsoever. Dangerous? Probably not as dangerous as having me in the mix with a snoot full of Sonata, I suppose.

Why would anyone snort sleeping pills during the day? Good question, although I don't have an answer that a nonaddict would understand completely. You should know that although Sonata is for sleep, it also has anxiolytic properties like Xanax and Valium. It works on the same receptors in the central nervous system as the aforementioned and more familiar benzodiazepines, but is not in the benzo family. In a nutshell, it produces a calming drunklike effect. That's what I liked. It produced the effect quickly too. As I was reviewing the details of the drug Sonata for this writing, I pulled up a page on the Internet with a picture of the capsule, and it made me catch my breath. My mind will still try to play tricks on me. Suddenly, after only looking at a picture, I could taste the powder on the back of my throat and feel the soothing sensation while sitting in front of my computer. Addiction is cunning, baffling, and powerful.

Throughout that workday, I had ingested several Sonata capsules via the nasal route. I didn't get totally wiped out because I can still remember going to the bar shortly after checking into my motel. I got to the Mark II bar about 10:00 p.m. I recall walking up to the bar and ordering a drink—bourbon and Coke. That's where the memory stops. My next recollection is waking up in the jail, feeling like a large truck had run over me, backed up, and did it again. I was in a drunk tank cell by myself. I knew that I was supposed to get a phone call, so I banged on the door. The deputy let me use the phone, and I called my boss, CC. His wife, Carrie, answered. I don't remember the conversation, but she came to the jail, paid my bail, took me to their house, and put me to bed in a guest bedroom. She told me to get some rest and come on over to the store when I felt like it and that CC would mind the pharmacy until I got there. This is enablement in its purest form.

I slept until about 10:00 a.m. As I showered and dressed for work, I struggled to piece together the night before. Nothing was coming to me. Then I began to start piecing together the story that I would tell Darcey. It would have to be a good one to explain my overnight stay in jail.

My mind was foggy. I was exhausted, scared, and sore.

When I finally made it to work, it was midmorning. I got some serious looks from the gang when I walked into the pharmacy. They weren't even pretending to not stare at me. Economy Drug was not one of those workplaces where everybody just keeps to themselves. No, these girls would start hitting me with questions as soon as I stepped behind the counter. I wondered, would it be Linda or Darlene that would start the inquest? There would be no hesitation though. That was for sure.

"What the hell happened to you?" was Linda's question with a smirk on her face. She held nothing back. If you looked like crap, she'd tell you. If you did something stupid, she would let you know. If you weren't doing things the way that she thought they should be done, she would enthusiastically correct you. After all, she had been there for over twenty years, and she pretty much called the shots. I didn't argue with her.

I answered, "I have *no idea*, but I woke up in jail this morning." My face had asphalt burns, my eye was slightly black, and I had shrubbery scratches all over my upper torso. I felt like hell too. My head hurt. My stomach hurt. My face hurt. My pride hurt.

"Where'd you go last night?" she asked.

"Mark II," I said, "but I don't remember much about being there."

As she picked up the phone, Linda said, "Well, let me just find out."

Linda had grown up in Pikeville, and she knew everybody. She knew the owners and the employees at the bar. I remember watching her as she nodded and shook her head side to side as she listened to the eyewitness account. Apparently, at closing time around 1:00 a.m., the bar employees were telling me it was time to leave. I wasn't ready to go yet and refused to leave. Mr. Large Bouncer Dude took it from there, hence the asphalt burns, shrubbery scratches, and black eye. Although I may feel ten-foot tall and bulletproof when I am loaded, I much more closely resemble a five-foot-tall rag doll with a big mouth and attitude. After pummeling me for sport, I was presented to the police guy who had been called on my account. Apparently, I wasn't ready to surrender to him either. This would be a new level of stupidity for even me. Up to this point, I had always given police officers the utmost respect even if I didn't mean it. According to Linda's eyewitness, I allegedly tried to fight with this one. He won.

The inevitable call home to the wife was my next step. My god, I dreaded that! I fabricated a story in my head. I had been waiting for my food order at the restaurant bar beside the hotel where I was staying. A drunk guy bumped me as I was waiting for my food, and then some words were exchanged. Things escalated into a fight, and the police were called. Her first question was, "Oh no! Are you okay?"

Yes, I was okay. I had fought valiantly against this drunkard and a couple of his buddies before the police came and saved them all from a certain beating. We were all taken to jail. I was a victim of circumstance.

I worked out my shift and drove home to Hazard. Thank God that Darcey was feeling sorry for me. I had pulled it off as the victim and would hopefully get some pity when I got home, maybe even some pity sex! She would see the bruises and scratches and maybe give me a nice warm bath.

On my way home, as some of the cloudiness began to evaporate from my brain, a question haunted me. *Where had that bottle of Sonata disappeared to?* I had it in my pants pocket when I left the hotel to go to the bar that night. I vaguely remembered snorting a couple at the hotel before leaving for the bar and doing some in the bathroom of the bar when I first got there. They were definitely with me when I went to the bar. That much I knew. I wouldn't have left them at the hotel. I would have left my pants before I would have left my pills. Maybe they fell out when I was fighting with the bouncer. Maybe I snorted them all and threw the bottle away. I started the day with thirty of them. I couldn't understand where they had gone. Hopefully, they had just gotten lost.

When I got home and opened the front door of my house, a frosty coldness rolled out of the front door. The ambiance had changed at the Combs's domicile. Sympathy was no longer the theme. I sat down on my couch and watched as my wife, Darcey, hastily dressed my two-year-old boy Cade in shoes and a jacket. I sensed anger in the air. She wasn't looking me in the eyes, and her eyes were black and cold and intense.

"Where you goin'?" I asked.

"I'm taking Cade down to your mom and dad's house because *we need to talk*," she replied.

We need to talk slid off her tongue as lava bursts from an erupting volcano. Her eyes glistened with fury and her erratic movements conveyed a feeling of extreme displeasure. Her head spun around in a complete 360-degree turn, and she was foaming at the mouth. Okay, well, that last part isn't true, but I expected it *any moment.* She was furious, and the talk we were about to have was a long time coming. In the past twenty-four hours, she had been talking to her counselor about the situation. I was *officially* in the hot seat.

My mom and dad lived just below me about fifty yards. It was the longest four minutes of my life. When she returned, she sat down in the floor across from me, looked me sternly in the eyes, and said, "I am not raising our children in this kind of mess. You have two choices. You can go get some help with your drug and alcohol problems, or I am out of here, and I'm taking the kids with me."

My jaw dangled only inches from our carpeted floor. My eyes were wide with confusion and disbelief. My wife had just given me an ultimatum. She had just threatened to *leave* me! The first thing that went through my head was, *Oh my god! Did she just say that?* The second thing that went through my head was, *How am I gonna get out of* this *one?*

After delivering her short oration of terms, she got up and walked out. I sat in my living room quite in shock. She had been angry with me before over such things, but this was a new resolve for her. I didn't want to lose her. I also didn't want to do what she was demanding that I do. Time would fix this. I would lie low for a few days and approach her about some kind of compromise where I got my way, and she didn't get her way. Master manipulator extraordinaire, I would weasel my way out of this somehow. I always managed—so I thought.

Her suggestion that I *get help* meant that she wanted me to go to the dreaded *treatment facility*. This was just not an option. I had already shot down the idea of going to treatment earlier in the summer when the family had their intervention on me. Darcey had given me a week to consider my options. God had other plans, and *he wasn't* giving me a week.

On Monday October 10, 2000, I came in early that morning for work. I was scheming the whole way down to Pikeville how I was going to get out of this legal situation. One of the girls I worked with was from Wheelwright and her dad was the mayor there. She was going to see what she could do because he had some connections in Pikeville. It was a misdemeanor charge of alcohol intoxication. When I got to the pharmacy, there was a spine-chilling surprise awaiting me on the counter. I will never forget stepping up into the pharmacy and seeing what lay on the counter before me. I almost vomited when I saw it. The hardcopy prescription for the pills I had taken with me to the bar the night that I got arrested was laid out on the counter. I froze and stared at it, petrified: *Why was it there? Why had it been pulled from the files? Who had pulled it?* My mind, in an attempt at self-preservation, conjured up all kinds of alternative scenarios of why it was there. I knew in the back of my mind though that it couldn't be good. My heart raced uncontrollably, and I began to hyperventilate. I turned these questions over and over in my head, and the fear was unbearable.

I took a 50 mg atenolol tablet. A beta-blocker normally used for blood pressure, it blocks the receptors that cause your heart to pound in fearful situations. No pill could slow my heart though when I looked up a few minutes later. On the front door monitor, I saw three men walking in. Two were uniformed police officers, and the third was obviously a detective. In a panic, I bolted for the office, which was located just off the stockroom. I was standing there when they came through the double doors into the office.

The detective looked at me and said, "Are you Jared Combs?"

I hung my head and answered, "Yes."

"You know why we're here, don't you?"

"I think so," I said, and I began to cry.

CC had known they were coming but had been strictly warned against telling me. He had tried to give me a bit of a heads up by leaving the files out.

The handcuffs were out and tightly secured around my wrists before I knew it, and the all-too-familiar Miranda rights were once again being cited. I was so weak that my knees buckled a couple times. I begged them not to take me out through the front of the store, but to take me out through the back of the stockroom instead. They did not honor my wishes. I was once again led out of pharmacy job number 2 in handcuffs and in tears.

I turned around and asked Mr. Cinnamond to call my wife and tell her what had happened. As they led me away, I heard Mr. C asking them when they thought I would be eligible for bail. He told them he wanted to help me in any way that he could. Mr. Cinnamond was a good man who had a place in his heart for me and my troubles. A couple years later, he died of a heart attack while working in the pharmacy. I never really got to thank him properly for all his help and love.

I remember thinking on the short ride over to the police station that this was it. My license to practice pharmacy was gone for good. My wife was probably finished with me. I was going to jail for a year or perhaps two. Although I had been off probation for a few months, I was still likely to serve jail time. I was terrified of losing my pharmacist license. I didn't know how else I would make a living. I didn't know *how* to do anything else. So much chaos rattling around in my terrified head, I didn't know what to dread the most.

At the station, I was photographed and fingerprinted. If having my picture taken wasn't bad enough, the idiot operating the camera forgot to remove the lens cap the first shot, so I got to do it again. Say cheese!

Soon, I was back in the Pike County Detention Center. One of the deputies noted that I had been there only days before. There was some discussion between two of them of my being a PFO, which could get me five years, they said.

"What's a PFO?" I asked.

"Persistent Felony Offender," the officer replied. "You'll likely do the most part of five years for this if you are convicted."

That would turn out not to apply to me since the other felony was federal, and this one would not be. I didn't know that at the time though, and it pushed me further into fear and depression.

I felt a lump in my throat. They took me to my cell and locked me up. It was a fairly large cell for one person. I think it was the drunk tank, but this was Monday morning, and it was just us *PFO pharmacists* in the tank today.

I began to pace around the cell to release some nervous energy. I would cry some then pace some. My thoughts raced through my head like a cattle stampede. I hated being alone when scared and sober. Especially while in a state of sheer panic and deep depression, being alone is the worst. There is nobody else to talk with about the pain, dread, and fear. Nobody to speak some kind words of encouragement. Nobody to make conversation with just to slow my brain. Nobody but me and my depressing thoughts.

Then something happened. The Big Book (*Alcoholics Anonymous*) refers to it as a spiritual experience. I refer to it as God's grace. *Grace* is defined as *free and unmerited favor.* I suddenly had an epiphany. "I am an alcoholic and a drug addict, and I don't have to keep living this way" was what came out of my mouth. A wave of relief followed, and I have not had a drink of alcohol or abused a mind-altering substance since. Amazing what God is capable of.

God gave me a willingness to change that day. He just handed it to me. I didn't have to give an offering, or do confession, or pray facing a certain direction, or go without food for a day. I asked. He delivered. Actually, he gave me a lot in that moment of clarity, but willingness was the key ingredient I desperately needed first. He also strengthened my faith. Not only did I suddenly become willing to do whatever it took to get sober, but I also truly felt that it was going to happen. I knew that God was going to help, like I knew that the sun was coming up tomorrow. I knew, in that moment, that *God could, and would, if he were sought.*

God made the offer to help me, and I accepted. Then I prayed, and I asked him to show me what I should do. That's how it all started. That's how I am able to sit here today, free from the bondage of drugs and alcohol. It's why I'm even alive today. It's the very turning point of my life. So many good things have happened as a result of the gift I received that day.

Faith is still something today that is hot one day and lukewarm the next for me. I find that to be the case with many people. Sometimes I simply wish that God would e-mail me directions each day. I don't always want to behave a certain way and guess at what His will is for me. No, I would rather get out of bed, check my Gmail from God, and find out exactly what I am expected to do for that day. Prayer and meditation in the mornings will do just that for me, but it requires so much effort on my part that I skip it sometimes. Life's busy. I have three kids, two jobs, and one wife. I'm rushing to make it to work every day. I just get too busy sometimes! I can make excuses all day. Faith is like a campfire though. If you just light it and go away, eventually it will wane. You have to stoke the fire and add more firewood to keep it going.

Christopher Columbus had faith that the world was round, even though many people argued at the time that it was flat. His faith was strong, though, in the theory of a spherical planet, instead of a flat one over the edge of which a ship might fall. He had three ships that he took on his voyage, and I'm betting that he was on the third one, *just* in case it happened to really *be* flat. I say that in jest to point out that even those who appear to have the strongest faith sometimes struggle.

I had been a believer for a long time. Church was a part of my life since birth, and I was baptized in the Baptist Church when I was twelve. But giving my life to Christ at that young age gave me no guarantees of a life without problems.

I believed in God even when I was using, but I didn't really want to make the changes that I was expected to make to be in his grace. It was kinda like I was telling God, "Hi, God. I'm gonna do my own thing here for a while, but I'll catch up with you later." I had drinking and partying to do. I went through the motions of the things that I thought I should be doing. I prayed when I really, really needed some help. I treated God like one of those fire alarm levers that you see at schools and stores. When the flames were lapping at my feet and the smoke was beginning to fill my lungs, I pulled the *God alarm*.

When they brought me some food in the jail, and I use that term very loosely, I asked them if I could be moved to a cell where there were other humans. I also wanted to make some phone calls. They let me move to another cell where there was one other guy and a pay phone right in the cell.

The guy in the cell was named Charles, and he was in for drugs too. He had stolen some things from his own sister and sold them to obtain OxyContin. He acknowledged he had a drug problem, but had no plans whatsoever for quitting. He made no apologies about stealing from his sister either. He was looking at doing something like nine to fourteen months in jail, and he had full intentions of getting right back into using again. He said he couldn't wait to snort another OxyContin. I never could understand that. People in jail usually at least have the good intentions of cleaning up their act or say that they do anyway. Not Charles. He couldn't wait to enjoy another OC (OxyContin). I told him that I was going to drug treatment and that he should think about it too. I told him that I was going to turn my life around and be clean and sober. I continued to try to convince him he needed help, but to no avail. It's humorous really that I was attempting to sell him recovery, and I hadn't been clean a full day yet. Later, I would discuss this with my mom, who reminded me that I had basically behaved the same obstinate way when approached before this day.

Charles had cigarettes. I was not a smoker, but I needed a smoke. There's something soothing about having a cigarette to smoke when you are in jail. I continued to bum smokes off him as we talked. When it was obvious that I was consuming a considerable amount of his cigarettes, I assured him that I would leave him some money upon my release in the morning if I got to go.

I made several phone calls. My family was working every angle that they could to get me out of jail. I called some people just to cry. I called some people to pray. I am sure that all these people loved paying for a collect call that costs six thousand dollars a minute from a whining, crying, babbling drug addict that just wanted to get out of jail.

The next day, I was packing for Cumberland Heights treatment facility just west of Nashville on the Cumberland River. I was beat-up, defeated, and ready to listen. I was scared, yet hopeful. Hope is powerful thing.

RECOVERY 101

So what now? I was off to Cumberland Heights to learn the basics of recovery. What I *thought* I was doing was getting "fixed." Kind of like a car in a repair shop that needs a new muffler, an alternator, or spark plugs. I thought they would teach me things to make me brand-new, or maybe tell me some kind of secret code. *Okay, team, Mr. Combs needs a new brain differential and a cerebral lube. Adjust his synaptic gaps and top off his dopamine fluids. Have the secondary team adjust his anger/serenity levels and send him home.*

That's not quite how it works. They will teach you things that *can* make you brand-new if you use them. It's not enough to go to the doctor and find out you have diabetes. If you don't use your insulin or take your medication and take care of yourself by eating right and exercising, you will continue to decline in your disease. Such is true with addiction and alcoholism. Our medicine is just a little different. Our medicine is a program of action.

We loaded up the Durango for our trek to Nashville. We checked into a motel the night before my scheduled admission. Sometimes I regret not going ahead and getting a liter of vodka that night and just tying one last good one on. My entourage would not have approved of that though. They had endured quite enough.

The next day, the intake person asked me lots of questions about my using. What I used, how often I used, when I had last used. They asked me about arrests and legal problems. Then it was time to discuss payment. I had no money, but I had Mastercard, which they graciously accepted. Later, most of it would be picked up by the insurance. My employers had kept me on the insurance plan so that I could have my inpatient treatment paid for. Initially it was denied, but the agent who was a friend of CC and Carrie and customer of the pharmacy came through with some influence and persistence.

After completion of the paperwork, I was escorted down the hall to the detox area. It was like an individual hospital unit, with nurses' station in the middle and eight or ten hospital beds in a half circle around it. In my room, my bags were searched, and I had to give up my cell phone. Then I was asked to stand in front of a camera that was attached to the computer. They took my picture and issued me a name badge that had an *L* on it for "long term." My picture was a vision of wreckage and dishevelment. Later, for my five-year-sobriety birthday, we would use this very picture to put on my cake as a reminder of where I had been.

Then it was time for my family's departure. I was scared, but ready. Hugs were exchanged. Tears were shed. And they drove off to Hazard.

I sat on the edge of my hospital bed, visioning the flowchart of my life, all the what-ifs, regrets, and fears. The uncertainty of my life weighed on me. I cried, but quickly and pridefully recovered when the nurse walked in. It was time for some medication.

I followed her over to a window like that at a concession stand and stood in a line of three people. There I received a small cup with a couple white tablets in it.

"What's this?" I asked.

"It's your phenobarbital," the lady replied. Phenobarbital is often used to detox alcoholics.

"I'm not taking that. I came here to get off dope, not try something new!"

"You have to take it. The doctor ordered it."

"The hell I do, lady. I haven't had a drink or drug in four days, and I'm not startin' a new one here!"

At that moment, the physician walked up to the counter, looking at somebody's chart as he walked.

"Doctor, Mr. Combs here doesn't want to take his phenobarb." It came out sounding like a second grader telling on a classmate for shooting a spit wad.

The doctor looked at me, cocked his head to one side, and said, "Okay, he looks healthy. Discontinue his phenobarb." He turned to me. "I'd like to give you a shot of thiamine though, if that's okay."

"That's fine. I just don't want any controlled substances thrown at me. I've been clean for four days, and it would be silly at this point to detox me." I resisted the urge to stick my tongue out at the nurse. It was hard.

I spent two days in the detox unit and then was assigned to the men's cabin. I hadn't really needed detoxing, but I had to wait on a bed to open up in the cabin. I walked across the campus and located my room. Two twin beds were in each room. There was a bathroom between my room and another room with two beds. The common area had several couches, some chairs, a couple card tables, and a snack cart with a coffee pot and a basket of fruit. I sat down for a while and noticed that all the guys were outside standing on the wraparound deck. All were smokers. Of the entire population there, I'd say over 95 percent were smokers. I soon found myself outside with them bumming a cigarette. It was social and calming, and most guys were more than willing to share. I didn't pick up the habit though, thank God.

I was one of the happiest people on the campus of Cumberland Heights. Several people asked me what antidepressants I was taking because they wanted to take them too. I wasn't taking anything. I just had hope. Hope is powerful.

Many of those same guys were in for their second or third visit. I became friends with my roommate, Craig. He and I had a lot in common, and we hit it off immediately. Just a few months after getting out of treatment, I found out that Craig had decided to go back to the crack pipe. I have no idea if he is even alive today. I would say chances are slim.

The campus of Cumberland Heights was beautiful. It was out in the country, surrounded by farmlands and trees, and a couple hundred yards from the banks of the Cumberland River. The food is outstanding. Most patients will gain an average of a pound a day. It was very clean and modern looking. Many of the counselors were in recovery themselves, which is always a plus for gaining the trust of addicts. Their traditional twenty-eight-day program, which is what I went through, offers medically supervised detox, individual and group counseling, AA and NA orientation, spiritual counseling, family program and family counseling, aftercare, and all the coffee you can drink. Although my only experience with an inpatient treatment program, I have to say it was top-notch. Did I mention how awesome the food was?

Rehab was very informative. They hit you with a bunch of recovery basics in a relatively short period of time, but it's an effective way to introduce the tools to somebody that really wants to be clean and sober. Even if they don't really want to, and many guys there couldn't have cared less frankly, it shows them a place they can come back to when they *are* ready, a place where they are always welcome. It provides them with some basic, yet useful tools that can come in handy later when they decide it is time.

My first evening there, we had a large AA meeting in the multipurpose room. About halfway through the meeting, I spoke up, "I'm Jared, and I'm an alcoholic. That's the first time I've ever said that in a meeting and meant it, and it feels good." It did feel good. I had accepted and admitted that I was an alcoholic. It felt like forty pounds removed from my shoulders. The group smiled and clapped for me.

My second or third day there we met in the multipurpose room where a Cumberland Heights alumnus who'd been sober awhile was coming to tell his story (affectionately called a *lead* in AA). The speaker had not been able to make it though. The counselor asked the entire group of about eighty people if anybody was interested in coming up front and giving their own testimony. I quickly noticed that everybody was looking at me, including the counselor that made the announcement. They were looking at me because my hand was up in the air. I didn't remember putting my hand up in the air; but apparently, I had because when I looked up, *there it was.* I got up in front of the group and gave them the story of how I came to be there. I think God pushed my hand up there. It was therapeutic to put myself out there, and also, it helped people there get to know me. I would give anything to have that on tape to watch today.

One recovery exercise I fondly remember was called *the ropes.* The counselors take you to a place in the woods, wearing a blindfold, where there are ropes stretched from tree to tree in a random fashion. Your hand is placed on the rope. You are told you have to get to the end of the rope. After wandering blindly around, holding on to the ropes for probably fifteen or twenty minutes attempting to find the end to this endless stretch of rope, I raised my hand. When the counselor came over, I jokingly said, "Dude, can you give me a hint or something? I need help."

He took me by the hand and led me away from the ropes. He whispered to me, "That's the idea, Jared. You need to be able to ask for help and let somebody help you." I have learned to do that today.

Another exercise had us calculating how much our disease had cost us financially. We had to add up things like lost wages, attorney fees, cost of treatment, fines, money used for purchasing drugs and alcohol, etc. I don't remember my figure, but it was a six-digit number. Seven years later, I wonder what my financial condition would be if I had not gone down this road.

There were all walks of life at Cumberland Heights. There were attorneys, nurses, teachers, and a nurse anesthetist. I met Christians, atheists, blacks, whites, and one peculiarly yellow guy. There were men, women, gays, straights, and undecideds; and then there was the mechanic for Delta Airlines. The mechanic was a pothead that kept forgetting which room we met in. Our counselor Barry would make fun of him and remind us that smoking pot would basically slow down our brain function and make us forgetful if not just plain stupid. He was a good sport about it and laughed along with us. He did eventually figure out which room to go to.

Some guys were there as part of employee-assistance programs, some had been court ordered, some others were hiding out from police, and some just truly wanted help. It was easy to tell that some didn't want to be there, and some faked it quite well. Some stayed, some left, and some got kicked out. It was rumored that a bar just down the road would give you a free drink in exchange for an AA token, which some apparently entertained. What a classy place it must have been. Sit and wait on the drunks to exit rehab and then give them their first drink free. Nice.

Counselor Barry was a recovering addict himself. He had done some time in prison for vehicular manslaughter. He had been driving in an inebriated state, accidentally hit somebody, and killed him. He had been clean and sober for several years. Each day in his class, depending on which step you were working on, you read out loud what you had written about this particular step and how it related to your situation and life. Then we would go around the room, and the guys would comment on what you had said. Sometimes they would agree with you, and sometimes they would tell you that you were full of crap. Each person got to give you some constructive criticism, and then Barry would offer his comments.

One day, we were standing outside the cafeteria after our class with Barry, and this skinny kid was describing an ecstasy high as an hour-long orgasm. This caught my attention. Can you imagine? As I listened, I found myself wanting to try this drug and fantasizing about it. I regretted that I had never had the opportunity to experience this. *Hmmm, an hour long orgasm . . . nice.* Then I realized that I should go away and not dwell on it. Today my friend Woodson reminds me that I shouldn't dwell there.

I made lots of phone calls back and forth between my family, my lawyer, and the board of pharmacy from a pay phone. The prosecutor was threatening to take away my license to practice pharmacy as a result of my arrest. I didn't know how to do anything else to earn a living and that terrified me. I liked being a pharmacist. Michael Moné, the executive director of the Kentucky Board of Pharmacy, said that the prosecutor could indeed seek to take away my license if he wished, but Moné said he preferred they leave the licensing part up to the board. I told my attorney I would be willing to spend up to a year in jail, if it meant that I got to keep my license—and I meant it. I had worked too hard for six years of my life to get that degree and license, and I wasn't giving it up easily. He was shocked.

My attorney was John Carl Shackelford. I have known him as long as I can remember. We grew up in the same church. We went on a couple of church mission trips together teaching backyard Bible school and putting on programs in host churches. We attended church camps together during the summers. He was, and still is, a very humble and respected guy. He was also my Sunday school teacher and agreed to be my defense lawyer for free. I don't think he ever accepted any of the money my mom offered him. He was one of the angels that God placed along my journey to lift me along.

Michael Moné, was the head honcho of the board. My previous interactions with him were unpleasant. I did *not* like him. He had a *Yankee* accent, and pronounced my name in a way that irked me. The day I was released from jail and on my way to treatment, I had to call him. I was crying and telling him I was sorry. He could tell even over the phone that something was different with me—I was defeated. He told me to go take care of *me* for now, and we'd work on the licensing thing later, and also, he assured me that getting my license back was *not* a hopeless situation. He could have shredded my license right then and there if he wanted to. I was already on probation with the board. From the board's perspective, I was a repeat offender that had broken a contract with the them and was dangerous to the profession and patients. His job is to protect the citizens of the Commonwealth of Kentucky from me. His response was pleasant and comforting though.

One call to home from treatment was not well received at all. Darcey was furious with me for something that had happened while I was away. Cade, at two years old, had found one of my stashes of Sonata capsules. I used to hide them so that Darcey would not find them. The problem with hiding drugs while in a blackout is that you don't remember where you hid the drugs. She had been on the treadmill and heard my mom yelling something at Cade. When she came downstairs, Mom explained to her that Cade had found some little green and black capsules and was trying to eat them. Mom had to pry them out of Cade's mouth. At two years old, he very well could have died or been seriously hurt had he managed to swallow them.

My experience at Cumberland Heights was a good one. My memory fails me when I try to recall details of my visit. I went there scared, yet hopeful and open-minded. Others I've met along the way have successfully been able to find and maintain sobriety without the aid of an inpatient treatment facility. I applaud them, but I don't recommend this route. For me, the sheer act of willingness to go was huge and opened me up to be teachable. Then the crash course in recovery gave me directions for a sober life. In addition, I was able to concentrate my time and efforts on me while I was there, without the distractions of family, job, or other extraneous hindrances.

The day came in November when it was time to leave. I was scared, but not terrified. I had watched others on their discharge date exit in tears with anxiety and dread of going out into the real world to try to survive. While I maintained a healthy fear of the temptations and challenges that awaited me, I was not terrified. I was grateful, hopeful, and composed. I was looking forward to being with my family again. I received my Cumberland Heights bronze token which read *To Thine Own Self Be True.* I said a few goodbyes, and rode out of town in the back of the Durango on a pink cloud.

Tricks of the Trade

How does a pharmacist obtain these drugs without getting busted? It's much easier than you think. A pharmacist that engages in the activities mentioned here will eventually get caught. Unless he just has some kind of spiritual experience in the middle of it and does a complete 180-degree turn and never looks back, he will end up busted sooner or later. However, one could conceivably do this for a long time before attracting attention. Actually, the best thing that could happen to a pharmacist in this scenario is to get busted. Consequences are a hell of a motivator for finding help.

Controlled substances are divided into categories of schedule 2, 3, 4, and 5. Schedule 2 represents drugs like morphine, Percocet, and Dilaudid. Schedule 3 contains Lortab, Lorcet, and Vicodin. Schedule 4 is your Valium, Xanax, and Ativan. Schedule 5 is Lomotil and some cough medicines. Schedule 1 are of no medicinal value and not found in pharmacies.

I didn't discriminate. I partook from each category. My faves were schedules 2, 3, and 4. The schedule 2 drugs are the most tightly controlled. They have stiffer penalties for diversion. At most pharmacies, they are more closely watched and counted. Oftentimes, they are locked in a safe separate from other drugs. Many places keep a perpetual inventory of these drugs, which means you inventory them each time you dispense them. For example, if I get a prescription for Percocet, I would count the amount out for the prescription, count the amount in the inventory, pull the notebook with the perpetual inventory of Percocet, and then make sure the numbers match what is supposed to be there. Schedule 3 and up are inventoried every two years by law. They are simply counted and recorded. They are not checked against any numbers. A pharmacist (or other pharmacy personnel for that matter) could take a small boatload of these without ever sending up too many flags. The problem occurs when one of several things happens:

1. In the throes of a growing addiction, the addict gets sloppy and lazy with the obtaining and using of the drugs. Perhaps he leaves the bottle of Lortab sitting out or puts it back in the wrong spot, and somebody notices the next morning. Or when pulling a dollar from the pants pocket, several tablets pop out with it and fall to the floor. Leaving deposits of white snorted material visible in the nostrils is tough to explain too. A couple of my mistakes include forgetting to remove the "snorting straw" from behind the ear after returning from the bathroom, and then finally forgetting altogether to go to the bathroom to snort them. I worked an evening clinic that sometimes wasn't very busy. I eventually would just snort the powder off the counter with just a quick check to make sure nobody was looking. Only there was a camera observing me in my case.

2. The addict's tolerance and dependence level increases. When we start out, we are eating or snorting maybe three or four a day. Most of us eventually get to where we are ingesting huge amounts of these drugs on a daily basis. When a person is scarfing down thirty or forty tablets of Lortab a day, it gets easier for coworkers to notice the missing volume. One of my ways around the volume problem was to spread my usage around different products. Any given pharmacy will have several products containing drugs like hydrocodone, which is one of the more highly abused pharmaceuticals. I would swipe a handful of Lortab on Monday, grab some Vicodin on Tuesday, then some Hycodan on Wednesday.

3. By this point, the mood swings and other behaviors are starting to show most likely. Family, friends, and coworkers begin to notice changes.

Stealing schedule 2s was very risky. One way to accomplish this was to take them from the patients that get prescriptions for them. Let's say Joe Bob the cancer patient gets 180 Tylox each month. If they are indeed a cancer patient or other patient with legitimate need of that many narcotics, it is unlikely that they would miss five or six of them from their bottle. It was important to know the patient though. Many people that got narcotics of the schedule 2 variety were drug addicts themselves. They were either users or sellers. That made them very likely to count their pills after leaving the pharmacy. You couldn't steal from these guys. They'd be back in the pharmacy in a heartbeat, pounding on the counter and complaining that we shorted them.

One other way to obtain some schedule 2 narcotics for personal usage is to empty only part of a capsule. Tylox was one of my favorites. I would remove a Tylox from the stock bottle and open it. Then I'd pour out about a third or a fourth of the capsule contents onto the counter or into some container. Then I could snort the drug, get my buzz, and the unsuspecting patient would probably never know. To take up space in the capsule, I would throw in some acetaminophen powder or some schedule 3 narcotic that wouldn't be missed. Some patients did notice though. I remember one guy coming in and saying that our Tylox weren't "fresh." I assured him that they were, but I knew that this particular guy was probably snorting them too, and he would notice. To keep from stirring up trouble for myself, I promised him that I would open a "fresh" bottle each time for him. What a nice guy I was.

Thank God that I am no longer an active user of drugs. Employed as a pharmacist in a hospital setting, the opportunities for procuring narcotics are ubiquitous. Frequently, one of the technicians will roll a cart up to me completely covered with narcotic wastage. Vials of fentanyl, morphine, and hydromorphone have been only partially used on a patient during surgery are sitting on this cart for me to shoot down the sink. How easy it would be to keep a couple of them for myself and squirt the rest down the drain. How easy it would be to keep all of it if I wanted to. I am the last one to see these things before they are to be destroyed. I never got into intravenous drugs except for that one time, but I would have eventually. Not to mention, these IV drugs are perfectly capable of being taken orally as well.

The first time I was subjected to this narcotic waste situation when I first started working where I do now, I ended up with a vial of fentanyl in my shirt pocket. I didn't really want to use. I wasn't craving. I just couldn't stand the thought of wasting a perfectly good vial of perfectly good narcotics. That voice in the back of my head that kept me from burning my own house down before came in handy once again. "Call your sponsor," it told me. I called Mark. He reminded me of all the good reasons that this was not a good idea. He was good at that. Usually, too, he could present this in such a colorful and logical way. I wasted it dutifully, and have since wasted many vials of narcotics without a second thought.

I'm not proud to say that I have taken drugs from cancer patients. I know now that it was wrong and selfish. There is nothing that I can do to go back and change the fact that I have done such shameful things. What I have found that I *can* do is stay clean and sober and vehemently stay away from that dark place of existence. I can carry the message to other alcoholics and addicts and offer hope. I can be an example to other pharmacists that might be struggling with addiction.

EMANCIPATION

Rarely have we seen a person fail who has thoroughly followed our path.

—Alcoholics Anonymous, Big Book, Chapter 5, "How It Works"

I left Cumberland Heights with a headful of recovery tools and a passion for staying clean and sober. I was happy and optimistic for the weeks to follow. I had no idea what my legal situation would turn out to be. I didn't know if I would get to practice pharmacy ever again. I just knew that the complicated, insane, painful way that I had been living had been brought to a potential end. No matter what, I didn't have to keep living in that hell. This was known as the pink-cloud period. This is the period of oblivious happiness directly after getting clean and sober and before life's challenges begin to surface.

Freedom from juggling all the lies I had been living felt good. The constant fear of getting busted by a wife, boss, or a cop can be quite cumbersome and complicated. If practicing pharmacy was out, then so be it. I would find something else to do. If we lost the house due to foreclosure, that's okay. Mom and Dad still had an extra room. Whatever happened, I didn't have to use. I had been freed, and life had been—for now anyway—simplified.

We sold the Durango I had won to a friend of mine that owned a car lot and we bought a Dodge Caravan that was a few years old. He gave us the Caravan and ten thousand for the Durango. The money helped us pay the mortgage and other bills while I was out of work. God was a few steps ahead of me once again, providing a way.

Eventually, after being home from treatment, the pink cloud faded; life hit me right between the eyes at a blinding speed. We call this life on life's terms. I was up and down with depression. I was anxious and fearful much of the time. I had no idea why I was feeling this way. I didn't know how to be a husband, a daddy, a son, or a friend. I didn't even know how to balance a checkbook. Like a long-tailed cat in a room full of rocking chairs, I was on edge all the time. I knew nothing about living a sober life. In the past, I had always turned to the things that instantly and faithfully changed the way I felt. I had always self-medicated whenever I felt the least bit uneasy. I was a fish out of water.

What I did know was that those good people at Cumberland Heights told me to go to meetings, so I did. I didn't like them, but I knew I was supposed to go. They told me to go to ninety meetings in ninety days, and that was my plan because so far, as they had reminded me, my plans hadn't worked out too well. Again, I didn't like meetings. They told me to go anyway. They told me to pray about it and keep going. I went. I prayed. I went every single day, except one day when I had a bad virus. I felt lifeless. It was one of those viruses that zapped all your energy and pushed liquid out both ends. I was struggling to get my shoes on to go to my nightly meeting, and Darcey said, "What are you doing, honey, you can't go to meeting as sick as you are."

"But what about ninety in ninety?" I asked.

"You can double up one day and make it up," she assured me.

I knew that if *she* was telling me that I should stay home, then I should stay home. Nobody wanted me at those meetings more than she did. I was relieved.

I hated being at meetings. I hated getting up off my couch and going there every day. I spent my time in meetings picking out the differences between me and *those people*. One guy would always stare up into the corner while he talked, and he would say, "Ya know," between forty and seventy-five times per share. I know this because I was counting. Maybe I should have noticed that he had been clean for a substantial amount of time, and I had not. Maybe instead of counting the "Ya know's" I should have been listening to the other stuff.

There were many shady-looking characters that went to the meetings. Some wore ankle monitors from being on house arrest. Without any tattoos, I was in the minority. Some would get up and go outside to smoke three or four times a meeting. I suspect that some of those were using during those breaks. Some talked too much. Some never talked at all. Then there's the person who would need to share at two minutes before wrap-up time and talk for ten minutes past the hour. I disliked them. I prayed. I kept going. I distrusted them. I kept going. I got sick of hearing the same old crap meeting after meeting, but I kept going.

One particular NA meeting, I met a guy named Mark Miller. When he talked, he seemed to know what he was talking about. He had been clean and sober two or three years. I thought that was a lifetime! Originally from Hazard, he now lived in Lexington. He told me that if I was ever down his way, I should call him and we would go to a meeting together. I told him that I would. A few weeks later, I was heading to Lexington, so I called him. We got together and talked for over three hours at an AA clubhouse called the Token Club. I told him most of my story.

After I would tell him a portion of my story, he would say, "I know." He did this over and over. I wondered what he meant by that. He didn't know me!

Finally, I said, "What do you mean when you say *I know?* I just met you. You just met me."

"Think about my last name, Jared. Who else do you know that has this last name?"

I pondered the question for a moment and it hit me. "You're Sherri's brother?"

He smiled and said, "Yep, I am. I know more about your history than most. And don't forget, I've been there too."

His sister, Sherri, was a pharmacist who had worked with me at my first job at ARH. She was also a witness in the federal drug case against me in 1997. How ironic to bump into this guy who would eventually become my sponsor and close friend in recovery. God has a plan *and* a sense of humor. He is still sober today helping others through opening a halfway house in Lexington.

At another meeting about a week later, I ran into a friend from high school that had a little-over-a-year sober. He was a couple years older than me, and we had played football together. He could tell I was struggling, and he pulled me aside after the meeting. He had gone to live at a halfway house called the Shepherd's House in Lexington. This was the second time I had heard about this place as Mark had gone there too. I didn't even know what a halfway house was, but as he continued to talk, an idea occurred to me. If I could get plugged in with a halfway house, maybe I could convince the judge that this would be a better place for me to spend my time rather than jail. Jails are notorious for having drugs available in them, and I imagined that Eastern Kentucky jails would certainly have that potential.

I got the phone number from my friend and called to get myself on a waiting list. They told me to call and check in every day to stay on the waiting list. I called at least once and sometimes twice each day. Through my attorney, I attempted to convince the judge and prosecutor to okay the Shepherd's House as my incarceration destination.

Before we heard anything back from either of them, the Shepherd's House called and said they had an opening. It was four in the afternoon on a Thursday. I asked them when they needed a commitment. I expected them to say by Monday or another day next week. No, they had to know by 5:00 p.m. today! Frantically, I tried to call my attorney. I couldn't reach him. I drove down to his office. He wasn't there. Finally, I made a decision to tell them that I would commit and be there on Monday. I figured that the worst-case scenario would be that I spend some time at the Shepherd's House and then have to go to jail anyway. A couple days later, I packed up my things and moved to Lexington. I would never end up moving back to Hazard.

The Shepherd's House wasn't what I expected. Actually, I had *no idea* what to expect. I didn't even know what a halfway house was!

Driving down Bonnie Brae drive, I was looking for a building with a big sign on it that said Shepherd's House. Finally, I pulled into a parking lot behind an old two-story house. I came in the back door, walking through a kitchen and into a dining room. There I met a round bald-headed guy that looked like the Mr. Clean guy in the commercials. The next guy I saw, Bob, had long hair past his shoulders. He was wearing a leather motorcycle jacket and reading a newspaper. Then there was Lonnie sitting at the table who had a piece of metal sticking out from below his lower lip, like an earring for the chin I guess.

What have I gotten myself into? I wondered.

I spoke to Lonnie. "So what do you do?"

"Play PlayStation . . . smoke pot," he replied.

"Yeah, but what do you do for work or whatever?"

"All I've done for the past twelve years is smoke pot, drink, and play video games. I don't know how to work. I've never had a job."

"Ah. Okay." At this point, I was ready to turn and run, but I didn't.

The inside walls of the Shepherd's House were a dingy yellow, adorned with posters of the twelve steps and twelve traditions. The ceilings were cracked, and a ceiling fan spun noisily over the dining room table. On the ground floor was the kitchen, the dining room, a living room area, a staff bathroom, and some offices. There was also a small bedroom for the evening manager to sleep. Upstairs was six bedrooms, which had two beds in each.

Upon my arrival, I checked in with James Hunter, the manager. I first had to pee in a cup for him. That had to be taken to a lab a couple blocks over. I just hung out in the dining room while I waited for that to clear. Then I was assigned my room. At the top of the steps and slightly to the right was my room. It was a decently large room with high ceilings. I claimed the empty bed and began putting my stuff away. Then I took a short nap before dinner. A short while later

I met my roommate, John. He had an extra pair of flannel sheets that he let me borrow. He made me feel welcome and at home. He had been there several months.

I soon was informed about the routine of the house. Monday nights, there would be a house meeting at six. That's where we just talked about issues affecting us at the house like rules, meals, and cleanup. Tuesday nights, we had an AA meeting at eight. Wednesday nights, we had group counseling at six and an AA meeting at eight. We all had weekly chore assignments, including cooking, kitchen cleanup, vacuum cleaning the living room, bathroom cleanup, outside cleanup, and a few more. You had to have your chore done and checked off by the manager by nine. You could pay somebody five dollars to do your chore if you wanted to. If you didn't do your chore or broke a rule, you got a check by your name on a chart in the hallway. Checks would get you weekend grounding if you collected enough. It seemed juvenile and silly at first, but it was effective. There was a clipboard where we signed out and in every day. We were expected to work a job at least twenty-five to thirty hours a week, and we paid $75 per week as rent. We kept a log of our AA/NA meetings that we attended and we were required to go to five each week. This direction and structure helped me immensely.

One evening, my first couple of days there, I was about to do my chore, which was to vacuum the living room floor. Several guys were sitting in there watching television, including the ominous Mr. Clean guy. I eyeballed the room and proclaimed, "Looks okay to me," and then proceeded to turn and walk out.

"Hey, new guy." A deep husky voice came from across the room. It was Mr. Clean—big, bald, and bad-looking with small gold hoop earrings in both ears and ubiquitous tattoos. He'd been there for several months, and this was treatment facility number 28 for him. He'd been to detoxes, halfway houses, and twenty-eight-day facilities all over the eastern United States. He'd been to jail more times than he could remember. His voice was stern, and he was scowling at me. "What's your chore?"

"I am assigned the vacuuming of the living room," I answered awkwardly.

"Then vacuum the damned living room. If that's what you're supposed to do, then do it."

"I didn't want to—"

He cut me off, "Don't worry about us, we've seen these *Seinfeld* episodes fifty f—ing times. It ain't gonna bother us. Just do what you're supposed to, and don't start off your stay here trying to find the easier, softer way."

He was right. It was my second or third day there, and I was already trying to weasel out on my chore. Not to mention he looked like he would just as soon eat me as look at me.

After getting turned down at all kinds of minimum wage jobs due to my felony conviction, I found a job at Hoover's Furniture in the warehouse. It paid $7.25 an hour. I had been making $36 an hour as a pharmacist. This was quite a pay cut and lesson in humility.

My first day at Hoover's, I felt like I had to prove myself around these rough-looking guys that were now my coworkers. The supervisor, Bobby, was the guy that had hired me by kindly *overlooking* the requirement that he do a criminal background. He asked me to grab a king-sized mattress that was leaning against the wall and load it on the delivery truck. Everybody was standing around the warehouse. I snatched up the mattress and muscled it off the ground. I spun, lost my balance, and fell with the mattress falling on top of me. The whole room laughed at me. I stood up, and Bobby was howling. I was so embarrassed.

"That's okay, man, that's okay. We do this to every new guy. Now let me show you how to lift these big sumbitches the right way." He smiled from ear to ear as he demonstrated a more effective and efficient way to lift a king-sized mattress by oneself.

A couple days later on the loading ramp just outside the warehouse, one of the guys, a four-hundred-pound black guy named Isaac, kept running his mouth and picking at me. I don't remember what the exact conflict was over, but it was basically just your typical test to see what the new guy will endure. I eventually told him he needed to *shut his fat mouth.*

"Whatchoo gonna do? Whatchoo gonna do? Whatchoo gonna do?" he repeatedly taunted.

"You're gettin' ready to find out, fat boy," I replied with false confidence while actually wondering to myself *what am I going to do.* This guy made at least two of me. His *belly* alone was bigger than me. It made up most of his mass. He tossed his hand truck aside and waddled over toward me. I began to imagine getting trapped inside his belly button after wrestling with him. Just what the hell *was* I gonna do? I had no idea! What I did know was that the Shepherd's House rules forbade any fighting whatsoever whether at the house or at work. Getting kicked out of the Shepherd's House was a one-way ticket to jail for me. What I also knew was that standing up to guys like this often shut them up and commanded their respect, but it had always been so much easier with a blood alcohol level of 0.25 or greater. Like a blimp hovering over a football stadium, he ambled toward me. I had made my decision to stand my ground. I was gambling like a big dog. I slid all my chips to the center of the table and declared myself *in* for this hand. *I'll see your four hundred pounds and raise you one, scared white boy.*

"Isaac, man! Won't you leave the new guy alone and go find some work to do! Go on! Get outta here!" It was a guy named Darren, my life preserver. Darren, also known as Big Diesel, had been at Hoover's for several years as a loader and delivery guy. He was black, in his late forties, stood six foot five and weighed about 320 pounds. He was as strong as anybody I've ever met in my life. I have seen him move refrigerators by himself and maneuver large oak entertainment centers like they were plastic toys. Isaac did *not* want a piece of Big Diesel, and he backed off and went away in a hurry. Darren invited me to go with him into the warehouse to help him load some furniture. I would ride the bucket attached to the front of the forklift and grab items that were up on the higher shelves. As we walked toward the back, he introduced himself. I explained my situation to him, and he smiled at me while explaining that he was in recovery as well, having been sober for seven years and active in AA. We became friends. God always seemed to place somebody in my life to lift me along the rough spots. Not to mention saving me from a beating.

Isaac and I became friends too. He was just testing me. I was so glad to not have to crawl my way out of his navel.

I quickly made friends with the guys at the Shepherd's House and became comfortable there. I went there to avoid jail time in the beginning. Eventually when I went to court, the judge accepted my request to do ninety days in the Shepherd's House. Thank you, God. Thank you, John Carl. Thank you, Judge.

Out in the hall after my court hearing, I saw the police officer that had arrested me. I only knew him from the court preceedings, as the night in question was still a complete blank. I walked up to him and stuck out my hand.

"Thank you sir. You saved my life." He looked at me like I had two heads. "If you had not arrested me that night, I would probably be dead. I would have gotten into my car and tried to drive. Thank you for saving my life that night." He nodded slowly as I shook his hand. I smiled at him and turned and walked away. He never said a word. I guess cops don't get that very often.

When my ninety days was up, I wanted to stay. I felt safe there. I slept well there. I was learning things there. I didn't want to move back home to Hazard and risk getting back into my old habits and hanging with old friends. I felt strongly that this was what I was supposed to do. I had a discussion with my wife, and we decided that I should stay. We had talked about moving to Lexington anyway, since it was doubtful I could get a pharmacy job back home when I got my license back. There's just not much of a market for pharmacists that routinely are escorted out of the pharmacy in handcuffs, and the wounds were still fairly fresh back home.

It was a smart decision. I needed that extra time to work on building my recovery foundation, and I needed to *not* be back in Hazard. I can't say enough good things about my experience at the Shepherd's House. I learned so much there. I learned how to live peacefully in close quarters with other people. I learned responsibility and accountability. I made many friends while there. Most have relapsed, some have died, and some I still talk to regularly.

Not everybody supported this decision though. Some family members on both sides felt like I needed to fulfill my fatherly and husbandly duties and bring my butt home at the end of ninety days. My wife was struggling to raise two kids at home, and they felt I should be there to help. I resented their opposition, but later was reminded by my recovery friends and counselors that these people did not understand this disease, nor did they know what I needed to do to establish a good recovery foundation. It was explained to me that I wasn't any good to my kids, my wife, or anybody else until I had a handle on recovery. My way had failed me miserably. I was ready and willing to try their way now. So far, this was working, so I would stay. Darcey, being the brave, strong, loving woman that she was and is, supported my decision to stay. I know that some days she questioned this decision and cursed my name as she struggled alone in Hazard, but she persevered and supported me.

Week after week, meeting after meeting, my loathing of meetings dissipated. It went from hatred of meetings to mild dislike, then from a dislike to their being tolerable. From tolerable, meetings became something that I looked forward to. My earlier prayers had been answered. I began to feel comfortable in meetings. I began to look at all the similarities I shared with these people in meetings and to stop picking out the differences. I stopped being an arrogant professional and let myself be a human, an alcoholic, and a friend to these guys. I stopped asking myself all the self-destructive questions: How could this work? Why does this work? Can't I do this another way? I accepted that it was working, and it didn't really matter how. My way didn't work at all. I heard in a meeting that it wasn't necessary for me to understand the physics of electricity in order to light up my room. I just had to accept that when I flipped the switch, the room would be illuminated.

As I stayed around, I learned responsibility. I learned about the power of powerlessness. I learned how to pray in the morning for help and pray in the evening giving thanks. I learned that doing just a few simple daily activities would increase my chances of survival. I learned that God wanted to help me, but he also wanted to hear from me. I learned that life without a buzz was actually possible, and not only possible, it was better! I learned that my life held promise that I could not even begin to fathom at this point of sobriety.

One of the first few AA meetings that I attended while at the Shepherd's House was a speaker meeting where a guy named Ryan was giving his lead. He had just recently graduated from the Shepherd's House. He was from my hometown, and his story stayed with me. The last day he used, and the day he had gotten arrested, he was standing behind a pharmacy with a sledgehammer. He was attempting to break down the brick wall of the pharmacy building in order to gain access to some narcotics. After a couple of fruitless whacks with the sledgehammer, the police came and arrested him. As he was being taken to the police car, he was smiling and laughing to himself. The cop asked him what was up with the laughing and smiling. Ryan smiled again and said, "Because it's over . . . no more . . . it's over." I knew exactly what he meant by that. I knew that feeling he was talking about, relief from an insane existence. When I was in jail and I knew that I didn't have to keep living the insane way that I had been living, I had smiled too.

I watched guys come and go. Some graduated the program, some relapsed, some just gave up, and some died. Some got high right there in the house.

One guy that graduated soon after I got there didn't last long after getting his own apartment. We had heard rumors that Bob had relapsed and was holed up in his apartment drinking heavily. My sponsor lived in the same apartment complex and rallied a few of us troops to show up at Bob's apartment to clean up the place. Four of us, armed with Formula 409, paper towels, Lysol and garbage bags went to his apartment.

We walked in the door to find this guy living in absolute filth. Trash was everywhere. Pizza boxes and empty liter bottles of vodka dominated the bulk of the trash, which was knee-high in some places. One of the bottles contained a suspicious yellow liquid we concluded was urine. Flies were feasting on the garbage and leftover pizza strewn about the apartment. He had pulled the mattress from his bed to the living room to minimize movement. The entire room reeked of urine and body odor with a slight hint of vomit. The guy looked as if he hadn't bathed in weeks, and he was smashed, bottle in hand. His face was red, and his hair hadn't seen a brush in days if not weeks. He basically just drank, ordered pizzas, and watched TV all day long. We washed all the dishes, sprayed down the counters, cleaned out the refrigerator, swept and mopped the floor, vacuumed the carpet, picked up several bags of garbage, cleaned the bathroom, and straightened up the living room. The apartment wasn't spotless when we left, but it was at least livable and smelled slightly better.

I didn't quite understand the point of our labors. I told Mark that it was a waste of time since the guy would surely trash the place again in just a couple of days. It wasn't like he was going to get sober and start keeping the place clean just because we cleaned it. He told me that if I stayed sober awhile, I would understand some day what we accomplished in Bob's apartment. Months later, I realized that Mark wanted me to see how this guy was living to remind me that I was only a drink away from that life myself. It stuck. I remember the experience vividly.

On June 13, 2001, I had my board of pharmacy hearing to petition for my pharmacist's license back. I felt confident. I had a clear look in my eyes, and I was there to tell the truth. I was clean and sober and living my life differently than before. It's so much easier to do something like this when you are doing the right thing and telling the truth. My recovery was real this time, and I had nothing to hide. I spoke clearly and honestly while looking them in the eyes. I meant what I said, and they knew it.

Once the board gave me a chance to speak, the executive director, Michael Moné, spoke up. "I'd like to say for the record that Jared has gone above and beyond what we have asked or expected, and

I have not seen anybody go to any more lengths to ensure a good recovery foundation than Jared." I am paraphrasing here, but that was the meat of what he said. I was shocked. This man that I thought was against me only months earlier, stepped up to the plate and went to bat for me when it really counted. It felt good to have people believing in me. I had let so many people down in the past year, including myself.

The board voted to give my license back to me with certain conditions attached, which would comprise my agreed order. I had expected the conditions as it was a standard practice. Here are the minutes from the hearing that explain the conditions of my agreed order:

> **Jared Combs.** Mr. Combs appeared to petition for reinstatement of his pharmacist's license. Mr. Combs was placed under oath by Ms. Curtis, Court Reporter. Mr. Combs gave a short overview of the cause leading to the loss of his pharmacist's license. President Conyers reviewed the recommendation of the Impaired Pharmacist Committee for reinstatement of license. Dr. Foster moved to reinstate with an Order of Reinstatement for impairment with stipulations as follows: probation for five years; enter into a HELP contract; attendance at either the University of Utah School on Alcoholism and other Drug Dependencies or the Southeastern PRN Meeting within one year; attend AA/NA meetings no less than four times per week; engage in the services of CDC/CDAC; no service as pharmacist-in-charge; no power-of-attorney; employment for no more than forty hours per week or eighty hours in a two-week period; random observed urine/blood screens twice monthly with others as requested by the Board; notification to all employers; notification to the Board of change in employment within five days; Board or Board President's approval of all employers; submission of a signed release for medical records; no dispensing of prescriptions to self or family members; utilize only one pharmacy for prescriptions; notification to the Board of all legend and nonlegend drugs taken within ten days; monthly self-assessments of progress of professional and treatment

developments; quarterly reports by counselors; semi-annual inspections and quarterly self audits at all locations or employment; required to live at Shepherd's House for first six weeks of practice; Order on Reinstatement to be drafted and forwarded to Mr. Combs for his signature and upon its return to be signed by President Conyers. The motion was seconded by Dr. Joyce and passed unanimously.

The stipulations sound like a lot, but it was just a few hoops to jump through to be able to practice the profession I love while reassuring the Board that I was behaving. I was grateful that they were giving me yet another chance. Most of what they were requiring of me, I was already doing anyway. I graciously signed the agreed order. Each month when I submitted a written self-assessment, I would begin by thanking the board for the opportunity to practice my profession. I meant it. I meant it from the bottom of my heart.

I was referred by the board to a man named Brian Fingerson of the Kentucky Professionals Recovery Network (KyPRN). The KyPRN is source of information for people seeking help negotiating their way through the discovery of their disease, treatment, aftercare, and petition for reinstatement of licensure. Brian is a consultant to the Board to serve as a liaison between KyPRN and the Board's Impaired Pharmacists Committee (IPC). He would basically be in charge of monitoring me during my five-year agreed order. I already knew Brian from my previous contract. I had previously equated him with the board and therefore the enemy. Eventually though, after getting to know him, I would call him my friend, respect and appreciate his counsel, and follow his lead.

After the hearing, I had planned on checking on a job that I had seen advertised in the paper. Samaritan Hospital was hiring pharmacists. I figured I would stop in, he would run me out of his office, and I would get to go take a nap. I already had a coat and tie on, so I called.

Grover Rivenbark, the director of pharmacy, invited me to come on in for an interview. I had been looking for hospital pharmacy jobs instead of retail. I felt like it would be a better place for me to be while in early recovery. In retail, it is usually higher stress and much more access to controlled substances. Hospital would be a brand-new practice for me and almost like a new profession, but something told me I needed to make this change. It was something I had dreamed of doing anyway, so I jumped at the chance.

Mr. Rivenbark introduced himself, and I did the same. He began telling me about Samaritan. Before he could get too far along, I stopped him. I had my baggage I needed to tell him about before I wasted too much of his time. I figured I would tell him about my history, he would get that glossed-over look in his eye and send me on my way. I was looking forward to taking that nap back at the halfway house after he ran me off actually. No hard feelings. Bed, here I come!

I told him that I was a recovering drug addict that was living in a halfway house. I had eight months clean and sober. I had just come from my board of pharmacy hearing and received my license back after a six-month suspension. Also, I told him that I was a convicted felon. Can you imagine interviewing somebody for a pharmacist position, and they tell you that? Heck, McDonald's would have probably told me to *have a nice day!* He continued to tell me specifics about Samaritan Hospital and the way the pharmacy ran.

"Did you hear what I said?" I asked him.

"I heard you," he answered. "As long as you're doing what you are supposed to be doing, you can work here."

He offered me a job. I couldn't believe it. What was wrong with this guy? What was wrong with this job? Fazoli's restaurant wouldn't even *talk* to me about a job only six months ago because I'm a *felonious* drug addict, and Grover here is ready to sign me up. *Sign me up then, Groovey Boy!*

In mid-July, I started working at Samaritan. I was intimidated and scared. I had never worked in a hospital pharmacy before. Although I didn't desire to steal or use the narcotics at my new job, my mind still worked overtime to develop ways a person *might* remove them from the pharmacy if they so desired. I quickly noted that most of the narcotics were kept under lock and key. This was good.

It was going to be like learning a whole new practice of different medications, different types of interactions, and different rules. I eventually caught on thanks to a lot of help from a pharmacist who had worked there for over ten years named Kip. Another godsend, he was patient, supportive, understanding, and one of the most knowledgeable people I have ever met. If it had anything to do with pharmacy, Kip could tell you the history, evolution, and present-day applications of it in excruciating detail. Not only did he know the drug's name, but he could also tell you the year it was discovered, who discovered it, and what blend of coffee they were drinking when they discovered it.

At first, I didn't like Kip. I thought he was a smartass. He lacked the ability to communicate in a tactful, nonpatronizing way sometimes. It wasn't that he was trying to be arrogant or anything like that. He just came across that way. One day, I was pounding away at processing some medication orders as I tried to learn the computer system. Two o'clock was cart fill time where we filled the medications into little drawers for all the patients in the hospital. It was a monotonous and tedious process that everybody hated and avoided whenever possible.

Kip peered over the carts at me and said, "You need to come and help fill carts. That's part of your job too." What I heard was, "Get over here, new boy, and check these carts, and stop hiding behind that computer."

I gave him a malicious look. I was furious! I thought about following him out to the parking lot at five when he was leaving to let him know that he didn't talk to *me* that way. *I've got some cartfill for you, Kip!* Who does that little punk think he is? He doesn't know who he's messing with! Early sobriety can be an irritable time. I was still at the Shepherd's House at the time, and I shared about the confrontation in group. My part in the confrontation was quickly and eloquently pointed out. *It **was** part of my job! Why did I have a problem with that?*

Several days later, I made a comment about my being late. Kip responded, "That sounds like a character defect. You need to work on that."

I thought to myself, *That's recovery talk.* I had never heard the term *character defect* except in AA meetings. It was weird. Could he be? . . . No, of course not!

A few weeks later, I was finishing up my day, and everybody else had gone home except Kip and me. I saw him fiddling with a small booklet. I recognized it as a Narcotics Anonymous meeting schedule. He asked me if I was going to a meeting that night.

"No way! You're—" I started to say.

"Yep, five years clean and sober," he cut me off.

I got chill bumps. It was an incredible twist of fate to have found a job working with somebody in recovery that had some long-term sobriety. That's exactly the types of things that God orchestrates so well. He knows *exactly* what I need, *exactly* when I need it.

We became close friends, and we laugh to this day about how I wanted to thump him for "disrespecting" me. We leaned on each other during some rough times working at Samaritan. Some days we would have a mini-meeting in the director's office if one of us was having a rough day. I know that God put a friend like Kip in my life for a reason. He was patient with me as I learned the new ropes of hospital pharmacy.

One afternoon, right before time for me to leave for the day, I had been working on a handful of orders. This particular patient had orders for twenty-nine medications. Upon finishing the order entry, I realized that I had put them in on the wrong patient. What happens sometimes is this: you start working on a patient but get a phone call from a nurse who wants to ask you about a different patient. After the phone call, you go right back to entering the orders into the computer, except you haven't gone back to the right patient. Stress, heavy workload, and inexperience can all contribute to such mistakes.

I was experiencing all three. When I realized what had happened, I almost cried. I said something out loud that wasn't nice and put my head down. Kip came over and asked what was wrong. I told him that most of the twenty-nine orders had been put in on the wrong patient. I must have looked like I was ready to snap, cry, or both. He took the paper orders from me, logged me out of the computer, and told me with a comforting smile to go home. "Don't worry about it, dude, it happens to all of us. Go home, and I'll take care of it." I was so relieved. He could tell that I was at my breaking point, and he happily stepped in and offered a hand. That's what guys in recovery do for each other, and it's an awesome thing.

At the end of August, I left the Shepherd's House. Darcey was able to sell our house in Hazard, and we found a house to rent in Lexington. I was anxious to get to be with my family again, yet I was anxious about being around them too. It wasn't the easiest thing to do. I was still edgy and, some days, just downright irritable. In October, I celebrated my one year of sobriety. My whole family came to the meeting with me and stood up front with me when I got my token.

My sponsor, Mark, gave a little speech before giving me my token.

"Sometimes as a sponsor, you come across a guy that goes to a lot of meetings, always shows up on time, does whatever you tell him to do, and just works the program like a champ." As Mark spoke, I cracked a bit of a smile and looked around humbly. "Jared . . . ain't that guy, but he's the one getting the token tonight, so now I'll talk a little bit about him." I gave him a dirty look as a room of fifty or sixty people across a smoke-filled room laughed.

The day after receiving my token, I began to struggle mentally. I don't know why it happened then, but I fell into a depression that would come and go for the next several years.

I resisted taking any antidepressants for the first couple of years. I didn't want to take any kind of drug. Many people, including my wife, strongly suggested several times that I should consider antidepressants. Finally, in spring of 2002, Darcey and I had a pretty intense verbal fight. I remember realizing several hours later that I had really gotten angry and overreacted toward Darcey. I called her and said, "Maybe it's time I made an appointment with my doctor and considered some medication." She wholeheartedly agreed.

Some members of the AA fellowship frown upon the use of antidepressants in recovery. To them, it is a crutch of sorts. I disagree with this viewpoint. This is a view generated out of fear and ignorance of the unknown. Antidepressants are not, in any way, addictive substances. Alcoholics need assistance with overcoming depression frequently, especially early in recovery. We have done some serious disarranging of our neurotransmitters while poisoning ourselves from years of drinking and using. We need all the help we can get to obtain some semblance of normalcy. Since scientists have found a gene that appears to be linked to alcoholism and depression, it would make sense to include this in treatment. It is helpful to find a doctor that is familiar with recovery to supply this help because frankly, in my experience, most doctors are pretty clueless about it.

Many of those of this opinion tend to be of the *old school* variety. These are the same folks that will run you out of a meeting if you dare mention anything about drugs in an AA meeting or identify yourself as an addict. I can feel the tension in the room when I hear this happen. They tout AA's *singleness of purpose,* which says that discussions in meetings must be confined to alcoholism only. While I appreciate this to an extent and attempt to comply with this for the most part at meetings, the fact is that today's alcoholic almost never deals with alcohol problems alone. Most of us combined drugs with alcohol, and excluding *any* mention of drug use is just not reasonable. The AA textbook was written in the 1930s when alcoholics were pure alcoholics. I agree that meetings can get way off track if we allow discussions to progress into detailed discussions of specific drugs (addicts can be bad for this) and other outside issues. That's really no different than staying away from mentioning specific brands of liquor during a meeting. Either would be inappropriate.

The problem I have with this rigid attitude is when I see tactless and insensitive alcoholics scold new inexperienced guys for wandering into an AA meeting and spilling their broken hearts out without using proper AA etiquette or, God forbid, mentioning that they smoked a joint. Some self-righteous jerks will confront these raw newcomers right in the middle of the meeting, interrupting them in midsentence. For God's sake, people, have a little tact and approach the person *after* the meeting to help them learn the ropes. Give them a break, and *don't* run them off. It happens. It's rude, inconsiderate, and it's wrong.

I'm stepping off the soapbox now.

My doctor started me on an antidepressant, and it was quite helpful. It also helped with anxiety. I know scores of guys in recovery that have benefited from them, and I recommend them when appropriate and under a doctor's care.

I needed that help, because getting sober doesn't automatically fix everything. It doesn't automatically make you a better person. It doesn't make you a better decision maker *automatically*. It doesn't instill you with the ability to be part of a successful relationship. When you take the drugs and alcohol away from the addict, it's a whole new ballgame. Take an angry, thieving, lazy alcoholic, and remove the alcohol. What you're left with is an angry, thieving, lazy person whose only relief from life on life's terms you have just taken away. I know some people in recovery that are as miserable as anybody on the streets sleeping under a bridge.

I had so much to learn. Alcohol and drugs had become such a big part of my life that I didn't know what to do without them. I definitely didn't know how to act. The more months sober I stayed, the more evident it became that alcohol and drugs had always been at the center of almost everything I did on a daily basis. One evening, I was making chili when I was just a few months sober. I felt strange. I didn't know why. Something was out of sorts—just not right. I related this to Darcey, who quickly diagnosed my perplexity. I didn't have a beer in my hand. Drinking beer was as much a part of making chili to me as adding the hamburger meat and beans.

My first sober deer-hunting trip was a similar experience. Drinking was more than half the trip to me. Everything else fell in place around the drinking. If there was no beer, but there was a herd of deer out in the field, my cousin Mat and I would have made a run to the bootlegger first, citing that the deer could wait. Maybe I'd lean out the truck and pop off a shot as we went by on our way to get the booze, but otherwise, we had our priorities to keep in line.

Now hunting has taken on a much richer tradition. My dad, my nephew Ryan, my sober friend Eric, and I all go hunting together with no booze whatsoever. We have an excellent time without alcohol, drugs, or hangovers. I look forward to the day that my son Cade is old enough to join us.

The first year or so of sobriety is full of surprises. Some are good, and some are bad. You get to a point though where you start noticing things you've never noticed before. This may come across a bit cheesy, but I began enjoying and appreciating things like a clear starry sky at night, a full moon, the smell of blooming trees, and the chirping of birds. I don't think I even knew that birds chirped before. That's what happens when your whole life and thinking is no longer centered on drugs and alcohol. When you're not concentrating all senses on using drugs or finding ways to get more, you notice things going on around you. When in the grip of our continuing and progressive illness, we don't see the beauty that surrounds us.

I can't say enough good things about living my sober life versus my old life. I could ramble on forever. Perhaps I have here already. Suffice it to say that life is definitely better in every area.

The transition from active alcoholic to sober alcoholic is a long and often frustrating journey. Some days, I wanted to throw it all away and take a drink because improvements weren't coming fast enough for me. One day at a time though, I stuck around, leaning on friends, plugging into the AA program, and praying while not taking that *first drink*. When a person is killed by an oncoming train, it's the first car that kills them. With alcoholics, it's the first drink.

RECOVERY, FAMILY, AND MARRIAGE

Having had a spiritual awakening as a result of these steps, we tried to carry this message to alcoholics, and to practice these principles in all our affairs.

—*Alcoholics Anonymous*, Big Book, *Chapter 5,*
"How It Works: Step 12"

The *Alcoholics Anonymous* text, a.k.a., Big Book, tells us that if we stay sober, "we will not regret the past nor wish to shut the door on it. No matter how far down the scale we have gone, we will see how our experience can benefit others."

My past is a selfish, self-centered, and lawbreaking story that I cannot go back and undo. If I could, I am not sure that I would since I have seen so many good things come out of it when looking at the big picture. Please understand that when I talk nonchalantly or even comically about terrible things like lying and stealing, it is not due to a lack of remorse or respect. It is because that is part of my past that cannot be changed or undone, and laughing and joking is a coping mechanism for me. I can only accept my disparaging past and go forward, making amends when possible. My life today is so rich due to the lessons learned, the host of friends made, and wonderful changes that have taken place. I wouldn't want to lose these things. Where would I be had I not gone through those storms?

I can thank my struggles for a stronger marriage, a better relationship with my precious children, a better relationship with my parents, a better job, closer friends, a clearer head, better opportunities, and most importantly, a closer relationship with God. If I had continued to drink and use drugs, I would not have put any effort toward pursuing these things. If I had not been forced into situations that were uncomfortable which made me struggle, I would not have stopped my destructive living. I would have stayed right where I was. Like a toddler in a poop diaper says, "I know it's smelly, but it's warm, and it's mine."

If you're reading this and someone you love is struggling with addiction, please do that person and yourself a favor. Don't soften their landing every time they fall. Consequences can be a great motivator for making change. If you are bailing them out every time, it is likely that they will continue to do what they are doing. Guess where I would be had I not gotten arrested when I did. Guess what I would still be doing if consequences hadn't rudely awakened me.

I should have died. I should have gone to prison. I should have been divorced.

I was headed down a road to destruction. My disease was taking me places that I swore I would never go. Had God not intervened in my life, the aforementioned consequences would be my reality. Yes, I believe that God, for whatever reason, singled me out and decided he didn't want me to die that way. I don't believe in coincidences. I have no idea *why* I am blessed with the miracle called recovery. I watch men and women come in the rooms of recovery and fail, over and over and over. They relapse, have consequences, lose everything, and go right back to the things that tear them down. No loving wife, beautiful children, promising career, or desperate parents can change anything until that spiritual experience happens. I was granted a pardon from my destructive addiction on October 7, 2000. Using the tools of recovery, I have not found it necessary to abuse drugs or take a drink of alcohol since then. I sit here today as pharmacist, husband, and father that has been in recovery from drugs and alcohol for over seven years. It has been an interesting and rewarding experience, which has left me a blessed man.

I feel very fortunate to have the opportunities that I have today. If not for a family that loved me through some of my lowest points, I am certain that I would not be here today. I would have either died as a result of using or killed myself purposely. I have been given many second chances and opportunities. The board of pharmacy has been very patient with me. Employers have given me jobs when most would not have even given me an interview. My family stood by me through everything. True friends were true friends.

My beautiful, patient, and loving wife, Darcey, has been there through some insane times with me. I'm not sure whether she loved me that much, or she was just too crazy and scared herself to get out. I don't think she could tell you which it was either. Either way, she was there to hold me when I thought I was dying, reassure me when the battle seemed like too much to handle, cry with me when I was scared to death, encourage me when I needed encouragement, push me out the door when I needed a meeting, and celebrate with me when I stayed sober another year. Today, she is my best friend. When I see something beautiful like a rainbow, a waterfall, or a newborn baby, the first thing I think of is how I want to share it with her, how I wish she was by my side. I don't know what I would do without her. She is a wonderful wife and loving mom.

It has not been all cake and flowers for Darcey and me in recovery though. For the first couple years, I had a lot of mood swings, and she held a lot of resentments. I knew that I was being an asshole much of the time, but I felt completely powerless over those feelings. I had never experienced a relationship without the aid of chemicals. We didn't know how to have a healthy relationship with love, respect, and communication. We fought and argued a good portion of the time. I didn't know anything about raising kids, being responsible, or respecting my wife. We attended some marriage counseling off and on. Sometimes it seemed to help and sometimes, not so much. Things got a little better for a while and then drifted away again. Not surprisingly, I had drifted away from my recovery program during that time, and Darcey had gotten away from doing the things that she needs to do in order to remain spiritually fit. As a result, from four to five years sober, we hit a wretched point where we basically just existed in the same house together. She literally begged me in counseling to tell her and show her that I loved her. I didn't hear her. By summer of 2005, she thought I didn't even love her anymore, and she was mentally preparing herself for our parting ways. I loved her, but I was in a bad funk and couldn't show her. I had drifted away from the recovery and spirituality that gave me hope and peace. I had become complacent and miserable.

Finally, through some intense marriage counseling, a couple of near fistfights, some passionate prayer together, help from some close friends, and dedication to each other, we managed to pull things back together again. We began to pray together every morning. We made a decision to put up a fight for our marriage because it *was* definitely worth it. The year 2005 was the biggest test of my sobriety by far. I am confidently declaring victory in our fight for our marriage judging by the past two years. We are a team again.

We have battles still, but they are fewer and farther between. One big key is that we have both learned how to apologize. That's huge! I know now that sometimes, it is best to keep my mouth shut. Often, if I truly feel that Darcey is wrong, I can walk away; and she will eventually apologize 90 percent of the time. Also, by walking away, I frequently realize that *I* was wrong, and I get to offer the apology. Apologizing is actually quite rewarding, humbling, and loving.

I can't imagine what it must have been like for Darcey living through the hell of our early marriage. She was constantly worrying about me dying of an overdose or car crash. She had to worry about me possibly going to prison for a while. She had to shoulder the embarrassment of my being arrested in our small town. She had to keep the bills paid and raise 2 kids while I was unemployed and away at treatment. She had spent years tolerating my drunken, slobbering, glassy-eyed existence. I can't imagine how lonely she must have felt. I am so thankful that she stuck around. I love her dearly, and I feel that we have something special that most couples never get to experience.

My kids are the absolute joy of my life today without a doubt. I have three beautiful, healthy, smart kids. My son Cade is nine. He is incredibly smart, creative, and sometimes a little stubborn (I can't imagine where he may have gotten that). He has a wonderful sense of humor and loves to draw and create things. If there's a tree nearby, he's going to climb it. He can do math problems in his head that most adults can't do at all, and he has his own Web page where he shows off his artwork and computer video creations. I coach his nine-to-eleven-year-old football team, and we have a blast together. He is very much like me, so I'm in for a ride. He helps me solve problems on the pharmacy Web page that I am responsible for called Bluegrass Pharmacists. When I can't solve an issue, I turn to him.

Kalin is our middle child at seven years old. She is beautiful like her mommy and happy-go-lucky. She sings much of her day through and is starting to show some real maturity and responsibility. She loves to read and probably reads on an eighth-grade level in the second grade. She is a daddy's girl. Recently, she sang a song with me at church. It was an awesome experience having her beside me up there singing a song. She did a wonderfully flawless job, which I did not expect being that it was her first onstage singing ever. I challenged her once to learn the locations of all fifty states on a U.S. map. I told her she could win a prize if she learned them via a computer program that I had found on the Internet, which gave her only a few minutes to place each state where it belongs. About a day later, at age six, she completed the challenge with one-third of the time remaining. Most adults can't do that.

Allie Grace is our little surprise from taking a couple months off birth control in 2004. What a gift this gorgeous, happy, curly-headed smile-maker is! Those blue eyes and curly blond hair thrown in with a devious smile will usually get her anything she wants. She's a mommy's girl, but she shares. Sometimes, when she's sitting in my lap, she will turn toward me and put her hands on both sides of my face and just rub her little palms over my beard stubble. She smiles and looks me in the eyes when she does this, and it warms my heart. She likes baby dolls, Dora, Cinderella, puppies, and anything pink; and she loves her big brother and sister. Allie has been a gift above and beyond all expectations. Regrettably, I didn't get to be a part of Cade's first three years due to my active addiction and relative absence from home. Nor did I get to positively participate in Kalin's first three years due to the insane nature of early sobriety. With just enough sanity and serenity during Allie's first years, it has been an absolute joy worth everything I have been through to get to be a part of these years.

Today, I would happily and proudly lay down my life for any one of them. I love them so much that words can't capture the magnitude. People that don't have children can't even fathom this feeling. I don't remember feeling that way before the changes that took place in my life. I would have told you that I loved my children, but it is clear that my priority back then was me. My relationship with my family is the biggest blessing that recovery has given me.

> *And acceptance is the answer to all my problems today. When I am disturbed, it is because I find some person, place, thing, or situation—some fact of my life—is unacceptable to me; and I can find no serenity until I accept that person, place, thing, or situation as being exactly the way it is supposed to be at this moment. Nothing, absolutely nothing, happens in God's world by mistake.*
>
> —(*Alcoholics Anonymous*, Big Book,
> "Acceptance Was the Answer," page 417)

The biggest and most important lesson I find in sobriety about my marriage is acceptance. It is a wonderful tool to use in any area of life today, but in my marriage, it is invaluable. When I can accept that my wife has imperfections, it gives me freedom. When I expect her to do things a certain way, I set myself up for an argument with her.

My serenity is inversely proportional to my expectations. When I expect people to behave a certain way and they don't, I am setting myself up for disappointment. When I expect my wife to do certain things without communicating them to her, I am asking for trouble.

The only person I can effectively change is me. We alcoholic/addicts are responsible for keeping our side of the street clean, and that is all. This is where the acceptance theme comes in. I can either accept that Darcey has exhibited a human trait and made a mistake, or I can continue to fight a losing battle and roll that snowball of resentment down the hill.

Early in sobriety, my sponsor asked me, "Would you rather be right, or would you rather have peace?" This was in response to my sharing with him of an argument I was having with Darcey.

"I'd rather be right! Duh!" I answered. Eventually I would figure this one out.

When I apply the steps and principles of the AA program in my life, I am a better person. When I take the suggestions given to me in the Big Book and the ones I receive in meetings and put them to practice in my daily life, I have some serenity. Suggestions are what we get from the book of *Alcoholics Anonymous.* There are no steadfast rules. There is no perfectly right way to do this program. The suggestions we are given are suggested to us just as it may be *suggested* that a parachutist pull the ripcord on his parachute upon exiting the plane. They are only suggestions, but they are strongly advised.

At about one year sober, I had begun to resent my wife asking me to do dishes. After coming home from working all day and then eating dinner, the last thing in the world I wanted to do was dishes. I was tired, and the couch was calling my name. We had several arguments over this; and finally, I talked to my sponsor, Mark, about it. I told him how inconsiderate she was in asking me to do the dishes after being at work all day, and how we had had several arguments over it.

"Jared, if you were in jail, would you appreciate being able to get out and stand in front of your sink to do some dishes?" Mark asked me.

"Heck, yeah! I would love to be able to get out of there to do dishes! I hate jail!" I answered.

"Then take your ass in the kitchen, stand in front of that sink, and do those dishes," Mark said. "Every night, I want you to do those dishes, and while you're doing them, pray and thank God that you are a free man with a house and dishes to do."

I still need to be reminded to do the dishes from time to time. I still need to be reminded to pray sometimes. I still need to be reminded to be thankful and to have gratitude sometimes. It is for these reasons that I need to stay active in my recovery and continue doing things like going to meetings, sponsoring people, and reading the Big

Book. I have friends in the program that will call me on my bullshit when I start to get out of line. They are quick to remind me where I've been.

When I'm at a meeting and I hear a new person sharing about how they just got divorced, lost their job, and they are only two days sober living under a bridge, my problems no longer seem to be so huge anymore. If I came to the meeting to share how upset I was that my big-screen TV wasn't working properly, I probably won't need to share that now. The fact that one of my pixels is out on my fifty-five-inch high-definition TV just doesn't seem to be worthy of meeting time anymore. I can go home and be grateful that the other two million pixels are working just fine and reflect on the quality of my problems today.

Recovery is a rewarding journey. I truly like my life now. So many gifts have come from being sober. I have learned to appreciate things much more than I did before. When I was drinking and using, I didn't really care about anything except getting high. My kids are at the top of that list. They are the joy of my life. I love spending time with them, playing with them, teaching them, reading with them, and watching them grow. I love doing things for them, watching them smile, and watching them learn. I love to cuddle up and fall asleep with them.

I don't have to always be looking over my shoulder, afraid of getting caught doing something. I don't freak out when a police car is behind me. My heart rate may increase a little because I can still ride heavy on the accelerator at times, but I know that the worst thing I'm gonna get is a ticket. I don't worry about them smelling some booze on my breath or finding a baggie of pills in my vehicle. I may have to go to traffic school but probably not jail.

When I hear the words *controlled substance inventory* at work, I don't go into a panic because I don't have anything to be scared of. If there happened to be controlled substance discrepancies, guess what, I'm not the one that took them! There's a lot of serenity for me in that.

When the board of pharmacy inspector walks in with his clipboard in his hand and that little smirk on his face, I don't suddenly get the strong urge to vomit with my heart jumping up into my throat. I just nod, say hi, and go about my work without immense fear enveloping me. It's really quite nice.

I've learned an expensive lesson about spending money. I don't *have* to drive a BMW just because some other pharmacist drives one. I don't *have* to have a Harley Davidson or a house in a certain neighborhood just because somebody else has it. It cost me about a year's salary, a few thousand in fines, fifteen grand in attorney fees, about ten grand for inpatient treatment, and five days in solitary confinement; but I'm sober, and I appreciate what I have today. I feel blessed to own a home. I have a nice home in a great neighborhood with great neighbors. It's not anything super fancy, but it's mine. I have a great job that pays me well and has tremendous benefits. I am however one drink away from a homeless shelter. You want to see somebody go from serenity to homeless in three point two days? Just let me start drinking or using again. I'll be in a homeless shelter or prison before you can blink your eyes. The board inspector will wipe his butt with my license before he flushes it down the toilet. My wife will throw in the towel. It's no exaggeration. I have proven myself.

There are times that an addict needs the aid of medications that are normally on the prohibited list. It is a very delicate and confusing situation for addicts and those that treat addicts. Even for those of us who have been in recovery for a few years, the possibility of disaster is but a pill away.

I've heard several stories in AA meetings where guys have several years of sobriety and then have some kind of chronic pain issue. The doctor carelessly, or perhaps unknowingly, writes a prescription for narcotics, and our friend is hooked like a striped bass in no time flat.

In the summer of 2007, I had my first root canal. It was some of the worst pain I have ever endured. I woke up in the middle of the night with a heavy pain in one of my back teeth. I had felt it before lying down and had taken some ibuprofen, but this was pain that laughed at ibuprofen. I took another handful of ibuprofen to give it something to laugh at and tried to lie down. I rolled off the bed onto the floor and placed my hands on either side of my head. I don't know if that actually helps, but it just seems to be the thing to do when one side of your head is throbbing like it is about to explode. Maybe it's an instinctual thing that minimizes shrapnel in the event that the head does actually explode. Anyway, I was rolling around in the floor in the fetal position, in tears and drooling everywhere. I had to find something else. There was no way I could stand this. It was about 3:00 a.m., and my dentist wouldn't be in until eight.

I got up and found some viscous lidocaine 2 percent in the medicine cabinet. I really didn't think this would help any, but at this point, I would have licked the butt of a poison dart frog to ease the pain. I squirted a couple teaspoonfuls into my mouth and tilted my head sideways to let the solution flow to the area of pain. Within a minute, I was feeling some relief. Oh, it felt so very nice to feel this excrucitual pain begin to lessen. I lay my head back onto my pillow to try to go back to sleep. Ten minutes later, I felt the lidocaine wearing off quickly. Like one of those mint pieces of chewing gum that tastes good for about twelve minutes and then immediately tastes like you licked an ash tray at Hooters. There's no interim; it goes straight from tasting good to yuck! The pain was back. I reached for the lidocaine bottle and took another shot. Again, within seconds, relief. I repeated this sequence until the bottle was empty. After the third round of it, I realized that I was probably getting close to an antiarrhythmic dose of lidocaine. I didn't care. I didn't care if my heart stopped. I just wanted relief. When I was down to my last 10 cc of my best friend, I tried to savor that last few minutes of bliss. As the last of the relief abated, I returned to my fetal position in the floor.

At 7:00 a.m., I took a shower and got dressed. I was going to be at the dentist office when it opened. I called on my way in and explained my plight. He said he was happy to look at me as soon as I got there.

It was determined that I was in need of a root canal. I don't know how they determine these things, and I didn't know what a root canal meant. I didn't care. He could have said he would need to remove my left testicle, and I would have let him. He numbed me up and drilled away. The procedure itself didn't hurt at all. I was comfortably numb. At the end of the visit, he wrote me a prescription for Percocet. I had already called my sponsor and had this discussion with him, and he agreed that with proper accountability, I could take them. I had learned from earlier AA meetings that people in similar situations had required narcotics for legitimate pain. I felt confident that this was an acceptable choice. That in itself means absolutely nothing. My addicted brain could conceivably convince me that shooting up some Versed is okay as long as I am using it for sleep. I had to run it by my sponsor and a couple other guys and my wife. All agreed that given my circumstances, I needed it. That was the accountability that made it okay.

The difficult part is that drug addicts are persuasive and manipulative. We have mastered these arts to constantly get what we want. Throughout years of drinking and using, we have honed these skills to be connoisseurs of master manipulation, one of our many survival skills. I could have probably convinced my wife and friends that I was in enough pain to necessitate some pain medicine. That's where they would need to look at some other behaviors leading up to that moment. Was I going to meetings regularly? Was I working a program? Was I isolating? Had I been acting different lately?

The initial root canal didn't work. I still had pain. It was explained to me that most people have three roots to a tooth, but sometimes, there was a fourth. Perhaps they had missed this fourth one. I endured a total of three root canal procedures before I was finally fixed. Somewhere between one and three, I had needed some pain medicine. Darcey had to call Dr. Lopp for me while I was in bed. Somehow they got on the discussion of my being in recovery. This was news to the dentist. Darcey got the impression that he was annoyed, if not outright peeved, that I had not shared this with him.

Brand-new can of worms opened. My first resentment was with my wife. I told her that if I felt like anybody needed to know about my situation, I would be the one to tell them. I was furious! She later apologized profusely. I am sure she was only trying to protect me.

My next visit to his office, Dr. Lopp and I had a little chat. "So Darcey tells me that you seemed irritated to find out from her that I was in recovery."

"I would have liked to have known that information up front, yes," he replied.

"And what would you have done differently if you had?"

"I would have probably given you some ibuprofen or something instead of a narcotic."

"I see. Well, the thing is this, Doc, first of all, ibuprofen would not touch the pain that I was experiencing. I have that at home and had already tried it. We talked about that. Secondly, I tell who I want when I want about my recovery. I happen to have been clean and sober for almost seven years, and I know how to take proper precautions in these situations. My recovery is none of your business unless I decide it is. I was just getting comfortable with you and your staff and had thought about broaching the subject, but I didn't want anybody to look at me differently. Now, thanks to my wife's indiscretion and your overreacting, I feel like everybody is looking at me suspiciously. I talked to my sponsor, some friends in recovery, and my wife about this and did everything that my recovery has taught me to do. Your reaction is out of line, and now I feel my relationship with the whole office is strained." I was pissed, and this is undoubtedly a paraphrase of what was said. I could have said a lot more. I have such a resentment against doctors that think they can't properly treat a patient because of their history of abuse. I understand they get a lot of BS from drug seekers, but I was no drug seeker. "Listen, I don't need your little prescription of twenty Percocet to have myself a relapse. I've got a whole candy store that I spend ten hours a day in, and I could easily get myself circling the drain of insanity again without your help. Don't kid yourself."

Dr. Lopp is a good man. He eventually did fix my tooth, and I am forever grateful to him. I just don't think he'd had much experience with people actually in recovery. The fact is most people have no understanding of recovery. He apologized, and so did I.

"One more thing, Doc," I told him, "please don't ever under-treat a person that is in legitimate pain just because you think you can protect him from his disease. If there's a pattern, that's a different story. If an addict wants to use, he's going to use. Don't think for a minute that you can do anything to stop that."

I could have probably presented things a little nicer. Perhaps I got on my soapbox when I could have kept it simple. The world of earth-people (nonaddict/nonalcoholics) has this view of us though, and I feel the pressure to change that intolerance, prejudice, and unfairness. Look out, world! Here I come! Yeeeeah right, me and my delusions of grandeur. Sometimes I think I just unload on people when I think I have the right to. I kinda make them my temporary punching bag, releasing a little self-righteous anger.

Cunning, baffling, and powerful is my disease though. I had myself a bottle of Percocet and a license to take them for several days. I took less than half of the prescription by the time the ordeal was over, but an interesting thing happened in the meantime.

At the point where the pain was getting tolerable and nothing like the initial ache, I still took a couple more. Looking back, I could have probably switched over to ibuprofen and been just fine. My disease whispered in my ear a couple times, *All this pain has robbed you of so much sleep. You need to go ahead and take one or two to help you rest.*

I am fairly sure it was this devious suggestion that convinced me to take one before bed one night. Yes, I had some pain. I'm not even going to try to legitimize or delegitimize my decision. Who knows where the grey area turns to black? I questioned myself the next day and didn't take any more after that. Soon, they were gone altogether from the cabinet. The little addict fairy came in the night and took them to a place where no addict can abuse them. My wife, being the good codependent that she is, apparently decided they no longer served a purpose and should be pitched.

My parents are getting older. My dad is now seventy-one years old, and my mom is sixty-seven. I thank God that they don't have to worry about me like they used to. Seeing your son in county-jail orange in shackles and handcuffs can't be very good for a person's heart. My dad has had bypass surgery years ago, and some stents placed in more recent years. I'm sure it is quite painful having to talk to your son through Plexiglas using a phone while he shivers from the cold of solitary confinement. No doubt it was excruciating for my mom to have to leave that jail and not be able to bring her baby boy home. I would say that watching me walk into a courtroom in handcuffs and shackles was quite painful. They don't have to worry about those types of things anymore.

I hope soon to have them move here to Lexington where I can take care of them and where they can be closer to their grandchildren. What a blessing to have parents that *want* to be near me and my family. What a blessing to be in a position to help them out now whether that is financially, physically, spiritually, or otherwise.

I am in the process of planning my mom and dad's fiftieth wedding anniversary. What an honor to be involved in the planning of such a monumental occasion! Ten years ago, I would not have been capable of being the organizer of such an occasion. I would not have been trustworthy enough to be in charge of the potato chips. I would have probably shown up drunk, with more booze in my coat pocket. I would have made my mom sad and possibly caused trouble. Today I can be a part of something beautiful like the celebration of fifty years of marriage of two wonderful people who happen to be my two wonderful parents. I am capable of showing my love and my respect for them without getting my selfish desires in the way.

My life and my marriage are far from perfect. I don't know if we will ever have one of those marriages where we never fight or argue anymore. Just last week, we had a verbal world war 3 over who was going to water the houseplant! I don't know if I'll ever stop making stupid choices that seem to set me back in my recovery. It has been my experience that when I follow the twelve steps outlined in the AA program that my life and my marriage seem to go smoother. I don't know if battles with mood swings and depression will ever completely go away, but it has been my experience that when I work my program of recovery, both of those things occur less frequently and seem to be less severe.

What I do know without a doubt is this: No matter how badly that I perceive something that is going on in my life, if *I add alcohol or drugs to the mix, it will most definitely get worse, not better.* I might get to enjoy some relief from it for a few hours, but when the sun comes up the next morning, I still have the problem to deal with—plus, I've jeopardized my life, family, career, and trust. Alcohol and drugs for me means a miserable life or death. I don't know for sure which is worse.

The problem though is this guy in the mirror that I shave with. Alcohol isn't the problem. Drugs are not the problem. My self-centered and distorted thinking will take me to a place of pandemonium and turmoil if it goes unchecked. My brain is so programmed from years of self-medicating, and it knows what can bring immediate gratification, relief, and comfort. And this disease will wait until the precise moment of vulnerability to begin whispering in my ear again all the lies that I believed for so many years.

The recovery program I work is not endeared by everyone. Some hate it as I did when I was first exposed. Some don't understand it, so they automatically fear and dislike it. Some think it's a cult. Some think it is weak to rely on steps and God and meetings. Some think all this higher power and God stuff is nonsense. As for me, I have found something that works. I am utterly amazed by the blessings that have been given to me by following just a few suggestions on a daily basis.

Attending meetings is the core of my recovery. I go to be a part of the fellowship. I go to hear people share their blessings and their nightmares. I go to carry the message of hope. I go to be reminded of where I've been and where I can quickly return to. I go because it seems to help me stay sober. I try to surround myself with the program of AA and men in AA.

I heard a guy compare being involved in the AA program to animals on the Serengeti plains. Migrating wildebeests traveling across the plains are often targeted by predators. The ones on the fringes of the herd are taken down and eaten while the ones that have situated themselves in the center of the group have the greatest rate of survival. I want to be situated in the center of the things that give me the best survival rate.

My church is a big part of my recovery. The spiritual portion of recovery brings me the inner peace and serenity that I need to go through daily life. God has been very patient with me and has shown me grace that, for lack of a better term, blows me away. I feel guilty sometimes when I think of the amount of grace that I have been given by Him. If you are a nonbeliever that is trying to get sober, please consider *HOW*. That stands for honesty, openmindedness, and willingness. Call it higher power or God or whatever, but don't close yourself off. Open that mind. Talk to a believer. Share your doubts with others and work through it. If nothing else, start out by saying, "If there is a higher power, I'm not it."

By being involved in my church, I further feed my spirituality. Probably the entire congregation of Victory Baptist Church knows that I am in recovery and that I lead a men's AA meeting at the church on Tuesday nights. The deacons and church leaders, I am told, often pray for me and my AA group. That made me smile to hear that. They think I am doing some special ministry by chairing the meeting. Selfishly, I show up and chair that meeting every Tuesday night so that I can stay sober. It's not some big sacrifice. I'm not some courageous saint that gives of his time to help others. I show up to keep *me* sober. If others come and stay sober too, good for them. The door is open, and the coffee is on.

My AA home group, called Daily Reprieve, is a very special group of guys that I love dearly. These are my lifelines. Each Tuesday night, we meet, share our difficulties and our joy, and have a few laughs as we take this journey together. We get together often for cookouts and parties. We keep in touch throughout the week via e-mail, phone, and text messaging. We help each other any way we can. Be it a recovery issue that needs to be shared or an entertainment center that needs to be moved, we are there for each other.

When I think back to my life before the change, I stand amazed. I had been the epitome of a selfish and self-centered existence. I am so very thankful for my new life in sobriety.

We all have a God-shaped hole inside us. Some of us spend years upon years stuffing things in this hole to make us feel better. We stuff food, drugs, alcohol, relationships, sex, power, money, and a thousand other things in there trying to feel whole and unbroken. These substitutes work for a while, but then they fail us.

Only God can give us the balance we hunger for. Only God can fill the hole with perfect complementary exactness. Let me be clear that I am far from being some saint or holy evangelist. I'm just a guy that needs help daily from a higher power in order to live a peaceful and meaningful life. *That one is God. May you find him now.*

DISEASE OR MORAL DEFICIENCY

This argument will be debated until the end of time, I suppose. I would have to describe myself as having the disease of alcoholism and addiction, resulting in a moral deficiency. How about that? I have definitely had my share of moral deficiencies, as evidenced by some of my stories.

What most people don't understand about alcoholics and addicts is that drinking and using is a desperate attempt to treat the symptoms of our disease. It is an attempt to self-medicate. And you thought it was much more complicated than that, didn't you? It works for a while and quite well, I might add. In high school and throughout college, drinking gave me confidence, courage, and self-esteem. It lubricated my inhibitions. I did some things while under the influence that I probably would not have done completely sober. With a sober mind, I probably would not go up to a guy that is twice my size and tell him that I am about to kick his ass. If I thought this particular guy was threatening my family, I might take a lead pipe to him sober, but otherwise a physical altercation would probably *not* be in my best interest. Without mind-altering substances, I would be much less likely to break into someone's house and steal things from them. Clean and sober, the chances of my committing a crime that will land me in prison go down *drastically*. Now these are all probabilities, not guarantees. I can still do stupid things sober. I've done them! Ask my wife.

One bright idea I had at almost a year sober was to burn down my own house to collect the insurance money. I knew guys that would do it for a small fee back home. Heck, there's a guy we called Big Chris that would've done it for a case of beer! One night in the

163

late eighties, we were cruising around town, drinking as usual, and I wanted some new wheel covers for my Beretta. I saw Chris, and I told him I'd give him a case of beer for some new wheel covers. He told me to meet him behind a particular bar in fifteen minutes. He didn't say *tomorrow,* or *give me an hour.* No, Chris needed only fifteen minutes to accomplish his mission. I waited behind the bar for him, and he was there in ten, with four brand-new wheel covers for my Beretta. So I had the connections to make it happen while making sure I was away somewhere.

I had lived in the Shepherd's House for about six months and had decided to move from Hazard to Lexington. I had a house I needed to get rid of so that I could buy another one. It made *perfect* sense to me. I was so clever! It was a stroke of genius! From somewhere in the back of my brain came a suggestion, a suggestion indoctrinated into my brain by my program of recovery. *Perhaps I should run this by my sponsor, Mark.* I called him while I was on a weekend pass in Hazard where the idea had been masterminded. I won't repeat exactly what he said to me, but suffice it to say that he thought it was a very bad idea with potential dire consequences. In addition to it being highly illegal to burn down a house and commit insurance fraud, he reminded me that somebody might get hurt. A firefighter may die trying to battle the blaze. The neighbor's house may catch on fire. All these things I had not considered. Most normal people would never even consider doing something like this. To my alcoholic mind, it was a dandy idea. Notice that the only person I was thinking about was me. Disease or moral deficiency? Until you have some personal experience with these things in the form of friends, loved ones, or perhaps yourself, you may not be able to differentiate.

Asked that same question only four years before and my sponsor might have replied, "Got some kerosene? I'll get the marshmallows!"

We seem to think differently as alcoholics. That's usually because we are thinking about ourselves. Who was I thinking about when I thought that burning down my own house was a good idea? Not the firemen. Not my neighbor. Not the insurance company. The actions inherent in the selfish way we think *are often immoral.* People on the outside, particularly those with closed hearts and closed minds, see only these actions and fail to see the potential in us—understandable, I suppose.

I struggled with the suggestion that I was self-centered when I first came into recovery. I could cite several instances where I had been selfless and downright generous! As time went on, sober time that is, the onion was peeled away; and I saw my intentions more clearly. Usually, I had some ulterior motive when being so "generous." I wanted, or expected, *something* in return. I either wanted you to think I was a big shot, or I had something in mind I wanted from you.

It is for these reasons that we alcoholic/addicts are often seen in a shameful light. It is the reason for the *anonymous* in *Alcoholics Anonymous*. And so it goes, we beat ourselves up and fail others miserably until the miracle happens.

A Better Way to Live

If I had been asked to predict the direction of my life in very early sobriety, I would have missed the mark miserably. Removing drugs and alcohol from the center of my existence has enriched every facet of my life. The struggles endured to get here have made me appreciate my life, and they have made me a stronger person.

Butterflies endure a similar strengthening as they come into the world:

> A man found a cocoon of a butterfly. One day a small opening appeared. He sat and watched the butterfly for several hours as it struggled to force its body through that little hole. Then it seemed to stop making any progress. It appeared as if it had gotten as far as it had and it could go no further.
>
> Then the man decided to help the butterfly, so he took a pair of scissors and snipped off the remaining bit of the cocoon. The butterfly then emerged easily. But it had a swollen body and small, shriveled wings. The man continued to watch the butterfly because he expected that, at any moment, the wings would enlarge and expand to be able to support the body, which would contract in time.
>
> Neither happened! In fact, the butterfly spent the rest of its life crawling around with a swollen body and shriveled wings. It never was able to fly.
>
> What the man in his kindness and haste did not understand was that the restricting cocoon and the struggle required for the butterfly to get through the tiny opening were God's way of forcing fluid from the body of the butterfly into its

wings so that it would be ready for flight once it achieved its freedom from the cocoon. The struggle was strengthening the butterfly.

Sometimes struggles are exactly what we need in our life. If God allowed us to go through our life without any obstacles, it would cripple us. We would not be as strong as we are capable of being, and we could never fly.

My existence no longer revolves around alcohol, drugs, and material possessions. Don't get me wrong, I'm not some spiritual poo-bah who walks around, witnessing to people on the street while smiling and handing out Big Books and Bibles. I don't live in a shack where I raise my own livestock and vegetables and churn my own butter while singing hymns and wearing consignment clothes. I still have the same desires for fun things. Some days, I want a motorcycle so badly that I can taste the chrome on my tongue. I love big-screen TVs, fancy computers and gadgets, and tools. I just don't worship this stuff. I still occasionally find myself doing things that I know are inappropriate and not nourishing to my spirituality. I get in ruts of life that steer me away from my focus. I think selfish thoughts, I do selfish things. I fight with Darcey. I judge people. I hold resentments. I use foul language. I steal crackers from the cafeteria. These things are still a part of my being; but when I do things that keep me focused on helping others, fertilize my spirituality, share the gifts that God has given me, and feed my brain with positive stuff, those negatives take a backseat and slowly diminish from being such a large part of my life. If I don't stay focused on these life-supporting activities and become complacent as a result, self-centeredness sneaks back into the picture, and all I can see is *me*.

Complacency is my worst enemy. It is defined as a feeling of contentment or self-satisfaction, especially when coupled with an unawareness of danger or trouble. For us, it means we get in a rut of comfort and a little lazy. Most of us at least go through a phase of complacency where we decide that going to one meeting a week is plenty, that we don't really need to do any written step work, and prayer becomes the exception instead of the daily rule. If we're lucky, a good friend will step in and be honest with us, perhaps slap us upside the head with a Big Book. Oftentimes this revelation, combined with a few small but palpable consequences, is enough to prod us back into a more healthy recovery program. I have friends that do this for me.

Sometimes though, alcoholics are not so fortunate. Their complacency starts with a few missed meetings and less fellowship with other alcoholics. Eventually, if we fail to maintain a fit spiritual condition, we start to slip in all areas. We start to tell *little white lies,* go places we shouldn't go, and do things we shouldn't do. It is a crafty and covert disease that is said to be doing push-ups during our sobriety, just waiting for a chance to take us out. Frogs and boiling water give us an example of what happens:

> A frog that finds himself in a pot of boiling water will quickly jump from the pan to safety. He may have some first-degree burns, and he may never produce any offspring, but for the most part, he's gonna be okay.
>
> That same frog, placed in a pot of warm water, may sit there even while the temperature is slowly increased to high temperatures. The frog's complacency allows it to sit there even to its death.

Don't try this thing with the frogs at home though. Frogs are nice, and nobody wants some PETA freaks camping out on our lawns. It's just an example of how complacency can kill us.

What we have as recovering alcoholic/addicts is a daily reprieve *contingent on* the maintenance of our spiritual condition. By staying focused on maintaining this spiritual condition, we are offered a meaningful and satisfying existence without the use of mind-altering substances. The immediate gratification we received from their use is replaced by a more powerful and more reliable source.

It takes what it takes to find this new way of life for some of us. For me, I had to go through some rather bumpy times. Some people don't have to go to jail or have near-death experiences to be loving, giving, and selfless.

My dad once shared with me that he believes it is his purpose in life to serve others. He feels that God has given him this gift of fellowship. He said selfish people that don't serve others are missing out on one of the best feelings in life. He thoroughly enjoys visiting with people and taking them a large batch of homemade soup or chili. He lives to build people up by telling them how young they look or what a good job they did or how handsome their children are. He used to raise a large garden just so that he could go visit people and give away his harvest. His life is one of simplicity and honesty. He enjoys a good meal with good friends, a sit-down in the living room surrounded by family, a twenty-dollar fishing pole and a quiet pond, or an opportunity to do something helpful for a neighbor. His belongings are very simple. This man has it figured out.

My mom always felt her calling was to introduce people to Jesus. She kept all the neighbor kids in Bible school and church when possible. She may not have rescued the neighborhood or the town, but she showed many people where to find Him when they are ready. She has always been family focused and has a hard time understanding women that want to pursue careers instead. She is not a worshipper of fancy things or a status seeker. Simple, loving, and honest is my mom.

Do you notice a pattern here? Both have the heart of a servant with God at the center, and they are happy people.

Somehow, the alcoholic gene filtered down to me through these two really phenomenal people. Somehow, growing up in a home of love, honesty, kindness, and selflessness wasn't enough influence for me to follow their lead. I needed to find some of these traits on my own by taking the scenic route, over the river of calamity, and through the woods of insanity.

Had I ended up in prison for ten years, I would be getting out right about now, here in the spring of 2008. God had other plans for me.

He lifted me out of the hole I had dug myself into and taught me how to live. Another fable demonstrates this:

> One day a farmer's donkey fell down into a well. The animal cried piteously for hours as the farmer tried to figure out a way to get him out. Finally, he decided it was probably impossible and the animal was old and the well was dry anyway, so it just wasn't worth it to try and retrieve the donkey. So the farmer asked his neighbors to come over and help him cover up the well. They all grabbed shovels and began to shovel dirt into the well.

> At first, when the donkey realized what was happening he cried horribly. Then, to everyone's amazement, he quieted down and let out some happy brays. A few shovel loads later, the farmer looked down the well to see what was happening and was astonished at what he saw. With every shovel of dirt that hit his back, the donkey was shaking it off and taking a step up.

> As the farmer's neighbors continued to shovel dirt on top of the animal, he continued to shake it off and take a step up. Pretty soon, to everyone's amazement, the donkey stepped up over the edge of the well and trotted off!

Message: Life is going to shovel dirt on you. The trick to getting out of the well is to shake it off and take a step up. Every adversity can be turned into a stepping-stone. The way to get out of the deepest well is by never giving up but by shaking yourself off and taking a step up. With God's help and a solid recovery program, we can learn to shake off the dirt, grow stronger, and go about our meaningful lives. We can live happy and fulfilling lives. But when we give up, get complacent, or pick up the bottle again, the dirt builds up; and we are eventually buried. Oftentimes, the pain gets so severe that death is a welcome finale to the defeated, overwhelmed, and conquered alcoholic. Going to meetings regularly helps us shake off the dirt.

As I sat in my kitchen writing today, I heard a repetitive noise coming from the living room. Out on the small deck off the living room was a bird. It was trying to come inside the house. I don't know what was so appealing about my living room, but this bird wanted in. The door is glass, separated into several small sections. I watched as this bird tried to fly through the glass over and over and over and over. It would hit the glass, fall to the floor of the deck, and get up and do it all over again. As I watched, I was thinking that the stupid bird would eventually catch on and go elsewhere. I said out loud, "How stupid of an animal do you have to be to do that over and over like that?" Immediately, I realized that I had been *just like that bird.* I got high, hit a wall of consequences, and got up and did it all over again the next day. I stole drugs, got in trouble, and, in just a few weeks, did it all over again. I did this over and over. Oblivious to an obvious pattern of insanity that unfolded in front of me every day, I returned to my glass, expecting it to be *different.*

ADDICTION AND
HEALTH-CARE
PROFESSIONALS

As an addict in health care, it would seem that my access and exposure to controlled substances would pose an insurmountable barrier to maintaining sobriety. This is not the case. I don't drool over Lortab each time I dispense it. I don't stare at the Xanax bottle and dream of the times when I used to snort them off the counter. If I did, I probably wouldn't be able to continue in my profession. A solid recovery program is required to keep from focusing on these types of things. Otherwise, it doesn't just go away.

When I look at those drugs now, I don't see fun, peace, and serenity. I look at those things and I thank God that my life doesn't revolve around them anymore. I thank God that I don't have to palm one while filling a prescription, sneak back to the bathroom, and snort it to give me a feeling of normalcy. I thank God that I don't have to roll out of bed, crawl to the bathroom, and snort a line before I can even think about anything else.

I have had days where I have gazed upon the Sonata bottle and hesitated momentarily. If it is anything beyond a momentary glance, my program of recovery kicks in. That is when I need to call a sponsor or a friend in recovery and tell on my brain. A prayer is always a good idea too. A good friend in my AA home group always says, "It's just best not to think about *alcohol*." Fill in the blank where alcohol is, and you can apply it as needed. As simple as it sounds, these are the things that release the addiction's grip on me whenever it creeps into my day. I don't know why these practices work. I just know that they do.

It is possible to depend on these tools only when I am maintaining my program of recovery through daily prayer, regular meetings, spiritual maintenance, working the steps, and working with others. If I get away from practices that keep me centered, you can bet that I will find myself gazing at bottles, palming tablets, and taking trips to the bathroom eventually.

The recovery success rates for health-care professionals are about the same as for the general population. People often comment on how they can't understand how I can work where I do as an addict. They say, "There's no way I could do that!" Maybe they could, and maybe they couldn't.

I don't know how it is possible for me to continue in sobriety while being surrounded by narcotics every day. There's no scientific answer to explain this that I know of. I don't really know how this recovery program works, or why it works. I am just convinced through experience that it *does* work. I have no idea what happens on a scientific level when I flip the light switch at my house to illuminate my living room. I just know that when I flip the switch, I get light. When I work my program of recovery, I get a reprieve from my addiction. It just works, so I just work it.

If you are a health-care professional struggling with addiction, you are not alone. That seems to be a common fear and misconception. Take the necessary steps as required by your board, know that recovery is possible, and do the next right thing. It can be done, and things will get better, one day at a time. There is hope.

Carry the Message and Do the Next Right Thing

While finishing up this writing, I received an e-mail from a girl that I have known my entire life. We went to church and all grade school and high school together. She was overweight, and my friends and I teased her constantly and relentlessly. It was a game to us, making her cry. It hurts me to think how cruel, thoughtless, and mean I was. It hurts me now to think about it.

While working the steps at four years sober, I came across step 9, which instructs us to make direct amends to people we had harmed wherever possible. This particular girl immediately came to mind. I cried like a baby when I contemplated and meditated on just how awfully I had treated her growing up. She was an unfortunate punching bag for me. I knew immediately that this was one of the most important amends I would ever make. However, I hadn't seen her in fifteen years and I had no idea where she was.

While visiting my parents in Hazard one weekend, I ran into her at Lee's Famous Recipe Chicken restaurant. We sat down at a booth and began to talk. I began to get nervous as I realized what I needed to do. I excused myself to the restroom for a quick prayer.

When I returned to the booth, I began the attempt at making amends. I told her that I had been very wrong in how I had treated her and that I was deeply sorry. I told her I would do anything to make it right. She was receptive and touched, and we both cried. It was an incredible experience and a remarkable relief. I knew that God had arranged this meeting. What I didn't know at the time was just how powerful the experience had been for her. Below is the e-mail she sent me:

First of all, let me just say that I am very proud of you for facing, fighting, and flogging your addiction. I know firsthand how difficult it is. I am a recovering addict myself. Yes, I admit it. I am an addict. My addiction to pills was short-lived. However, my addiction to alcohol has nearly been my downfall. I am working hard but it is certainly an uphill battle. I admire what you are doing and just wanted to let you know how proud I am of you. I have never gotten over our conversation in Lee's that day when we discussed our past and your amends list. Your apology and how humble you were was enlightening. That meant more to me than you will ever know, and I have many, many times referred to that conversation in my mind during difficult times in my addiction. You have been an inspiration to me during my recovery and you didn't even know it. I thought it was important that you know. Someone mentioned that you had written a book. I would LOVE to purchase one if that is possible. I am sure it will be a source of strength and comfort to me throughout my recovery. No one quite knows the darkness and hell of addiction unless they have lived it. Reading words of someone that has not only been through it, but someone that is also a life-long friend whom I respect and admire would be a great deal of help to me. Thank you for putting yourself out there to help others. Being candid will most assuredly be of great assistance to many people, including myself.

That is what makes it all worthwhile right there. On those days when it seems like everything else is wrong and the only thing I do right is *not drink or use drugs*, I will reflect on those words and do the next right thing.

The Happy Ending . . . and Beginning

I have a life today. I have a real life with a real marriage, real friends, and real relationships. My kids like me. I am employable. I get to feel joy, and I get to feel pain. I get to have nice easy days where my job goes well, the traffic lights cooperate with me, and my kids are behaving when I get home. I also get to have days where I question whether or not I should have gotten out of bed. I get to participate in life instead of struggling day after day while life passes me by. What a blessing!

Today, I'm not out drinking and driving and endangering people's lives that are on the road. I'm not endangering my own kids' lives by driving them around while intoxicated. My patients will not be in danger of mistakes made because their pharmacist is in a blackout. I'm not stealing narcotics from terminal-cancer patients that desperately need them. My parents and my wife can go to sleep at night and not worry about whether I will make it home or not. Today, there is some serenity surrounding my life. Today, I *live* my life instead of just trying to survive it.

I pray that this book brings hope to at least one person that is struggling with alcoholism or addiction. If just one person receives that message and reaches out for this sober life, the hours spent writing and rewriting this book will have been worth it. Whether you're in the medical profession or not, a sober life is possible. I don't claim to know the secret to getting clean and sober and staying that way, but I do know that if you're willing to go to any length, there's hope. If you're sick and tired of being sick and tired, congratulations; you're in a good place. Help is available, and there are literally thousands of people willing to reach out and show you

176

the way. I don't claim that AA is the only way to find sobriety, but it's the way *I* found sobriety. By going to meetings, reading the Big Book, working with others to carry the message, praying, and working with a sponsor, I get to stay sober one day at a time. That seems to be the magic formula for me. Your formula may be different. Just get *a* formula.

Today is a good day. It is Friday, and school is out for the kids due to an ice storm. I will get to hang out with my babies and probably go to an afternoon AA meeting to shake off a little dirt. I've driven in worse conditions to get to liquor stores, so I'll be just fine driving slowly to get to my AA meeting. There, I will hang out with guys that are walking my same path. I will see men that I consider true friends. Many of these guys would get out of bed at two or three in the morning and come to me without hesitation if I needed their help. These are guys that routinely call me and ask how I am doing today. Later I will spend time with my kids watching a movie, playing a game, or making cookies. Perhaps Cade and I will make a new video on the computer. Kalin and I may grab our books and read quietly together. Allie Grace will no doubt want me to read a book to her and Sparkle Bear, her favorite stuffed animal. I will cook dinner and eat with my family. I will read some, and I will write some. If possible with three kids and two dogs, I will spend some adult time with my beautiful wife, Darcey—translate that how you will. At the end of the day, I will go to bed fairly early, in a warm, quiet home. This is what I consider a good day today, soberly spending time with family and staying *out* of chaos, insanity, and trouble.

INDEX

CPSIA information can be obtained at www.ICGtesting.com
Printed in the USA
BVOW072103241011

274416BV00002B/50/P